How to
Win Friends
and
Influenza

Edward Kurtz

To

CANDICE

ENJOY

GOD BLESS

E Kurtz

Editing and cover design
by
Silk Purse Editorial Services
Chester, New York

How to Win Friends and Influenza
ISBN: 0-9744322-0-2

Published by:
Westview Publishing, Inc.
8120 Sawyer Brown Road, Suite 107
P.O. Box 210183
Nashville, TN 37221
(615) 646-6141
www.westviewpublishing.com

Ed Kurtz in World War II

About the Author

Edward Kurtz is a lifelong resident of New Jersey. At 18 he went to work for the Forstmann Woolen Co. in Garfield as an oiler boy, and rose to quality control supervisor. When the mill closed, he formed a house painting business.

At 21, Ed organized a Cadet Corps of 35 boys in Clifton. During the Second World War he enlisted in the Army Signal Corps, spending one year at Camp Crowder, Mo., and subsequently serving overseas in five countries as an instructor in radio communications. He holds an amateur extra class radio license.

Ed has served the Boy Scouts of America as a scoutmaster since 1940. He has earned the Silver Beaver award and is still active in scouting. He also started a Junior Achievement group in Passaic.

Ed Kurtz has a son, Paul. Ed retired at 87, and lives in Clifton with his 93-year-old sister, Mitzie.

Introduction

After working hard, entangled in a sea of paperwork, writing and rewriting, I often wondered how I ever became obsessed with such a project as this. Then the other day I learned the power of the pen—when it leaked in my pocket.

I started my manuscript several years ago, dictating to my sister Mitzie, who would write the material by hand.

My main object in writing this book is to compare our mode of living over a span of one hundred years or more, since my parents arrived on Ellis Island in the 1890s, and how we lived without the frivolities of today's world. I look back and wonder how we existed with the few things we were accustomed to.

I also feel that few sportspeople know the origin of their sports. All my life I have played sports, and never questioned their origin. After I did my research, I was pleased to learn just how it all started.

A Great Adventure

Scientists believe that our world is between two and three billion years old. Some people can't imagine that this planet revolves around the sun. In the old days, let's say in the beginning of human intelligence, it was assumed that the world was flat, and that a ship would fall off if it went too far out to sea. (When I read this story in my history books it seemed so silly--but after some thought, I still do not go too far from home.)

We have established that the first aliens to inhabit the earth were Adam and Eve. Most religions believe that these two souls were created in the garden of Eden. So be it. The story begins with Adam, Eve, the snake, and the apple (also a worm--every apple must have a worm.) This epic was handed down by the wise men. Archeologists continue to dig and find many biblical artifacts that can prove the bible is true.

This story begins more than one hundred years ago, when my parents arrived on separate ships from Hungary around 1894.

All immigrants entering the United States came through Ellis Island, a small island in New York harbor, one mile south of the Battery, which replaced the old immigration center at Castle Garden. The U.S. immigration commissioner had his office on this island, and immigrants were detained, in compliance with the immigration laws, until deported or allowed to enter the United States. The move to America was not a religious drive. The overwhelming majority of immigrants were driven to this country as a result of economic force. This was called "old immigration."

This group gave America its Anglo-Saxon quality. It came in search of a new home in this country where free land could be had, thus building an agricultural civilization.

After my parents each established themselves, they met in Passaic, N.J. Due to difficult conditions, my father, still single, had moved to Phillipsburg, N.J., where he worked in a quarry. But he later visited Passaic, and this is where romance began. He happened to attend a dance in Passaic, and while dancing there he said to his friend, "Who is that pretty little girl, flitting around dancing with her girl friend?" My mother was then only 16. My father became very interested, and said to his friend, "Some day I will marry that pretty little girl." And a few years later, he did.

Married, they lived struggling ever after (just punning).

Three children were born, two boys and a girl, there in Phillipsburg. Three years later, the little family moved to Garfield, N.J. Later the family increased by another boy and girl. The family of seven lived in a small house, and "mother knew best" how to manage the hungry gang.

This small house is where we started as children, where the whole story began.

The house has not changed. As a matter of fact, the house was moved from an area in Allwoood, N.J. that is now the Clifton Extension. The house is now located on Madeline Avenue, which is parallel to Lanza Avenue, in Garfield.

All seven of us occupied that house, which was built upon a basement made of cinder blocks. We were well organized. Mom set the program for each of us, and there was no "Don't bother me" nonsense. This is very exciting, especially for today's young who have no idea of the method used to maintain a group like this.

Let's all get on the magic carpet, which was called a "runabout." Follow me through the house. The kitchen contained a large coal stove, which was the only source of heating the house. The china closet, or cupboard, contained other things of useful nature, like the penny jar, dishes--and oh yes, don't forget the cookie jar.

Refrigeration? To us it was a strange word. The freezer did not exist. Dearly beloved, the ice box was about the size of a small refrigerator, with an area to receive a small block of ice. When the ice began to melt, the water ran through a pipe under the ice box and into a pan. If the pan was not attended to, the water ran onto the floor. That's how we always had clean floors. Some genius invented an extension pipe to fit under the ice box, which emptied into a cellar tub. The ice was never frozen enough to preserve food as the fridge does today. We only added food that would not perish. Some people tried to preserve the ice by wrapping it in newspaper. They didn't understand that this ice would not cool the food.

Ice houses appeared in strategic parts of the city. These were storage places for the cut ice blocks, until they were delivered to the homes. It was interesting to see how they cut the blocks of ice from the frozen ponds and lakes. The attendant told me that the surface of the ice on these ponds and lakes must be cleared by scrapers. He said, "Note how we outline the ice for the cuts required." This was done by a machine called a "marker," which I noticed was drawn by mules. Should we complain today?

At the homes, a card was placed in the window. On each corner was a designated amount, 10 cents, 15 cents, 25 cents, and so on. The iceman would cut the required size and deliver it using large metal tongs.

We enjoyed the iceman and his horse, and told him his horse was a beautiful animal that should be taken to the track as a racer. The iceman let us watch his horse, and for that we received large chunks of ice to lick.

The kitchen had no fireplace, but it contained a large table where all the requirements were available. As for the stove, the only "Magic Chef" was my mother. Now picture five hungry kids who know how to eat. The kitchen was the all-around meeting place, and when we had visitors, they sat in the kitchen while we kids were not permitted to attend, according to the old proverb, "Children should be seen and not heard." The highlight of the stove was the intense method of cleaning with polish until it sparkled.

We had coal delivered through chutes placed into the basement windows. If they could not reach the window, the coalmen carried it in bags on their shoulders, or in bushel baskets. The cellars or basements were divided to hold the coal, which we carried up to the kitchen coal stove.

And how did all seven of us sleep? There were two bedrooms upstairs, and the rest of the rooms were downstairs, including a cellar or basement. During cold weather there was no heat after the stove went out, but we had thick featherbeds that kept us warm until it was time to start the fire in the coal stove again.

Laundry was a difficult job. Water was poured into a large vat and placed on the stove When the water was hot, we grasped the two handles and poured it into the washtub. Here was the famous "rub-a-dub-dub" and lots of elbow grease. This rubbing was done on a serrated washboard. Next the clothes were rinsed and some bluing was added to make them really white. Then they were ready to hang on the clothes line outside. Boy, on a windy day the sheets flew about as if they were sails on a ship. Interested neighbors would eye the clothes on our line, which included men's underwear where the rear end contained buttons that would enable the men to do their duty, since winter underwear was made in one piece. One had to be quick on the draw to maintain tranquility.

We collected the rain water in large buckets outside, and used this pure water to wash. It was excellent for washing your hair. We had an ingenious method of bathing, especially for the children. We had round or oblong tubs, heated up the water on the stove, poured it into the tub on the floor, sat in it, and washed away. We splashed and enjoyed the whole trip, even though some soap got into our eyes. Mom would get the giant towel and wipe us down, and now we were ready for bed. Mom said, Scoot away to bed, and don't forget your prayers.

The way to execute a chicken for food purposes was to place the chicken on a block, and position its neck so as to cut the head off. The headless chicken ran around for a while, and was then stripped of its feathers. But the hangman at times would indulge in a few spirits, and the blows were not too accurate, resulting in some deep cuts. In the old days, many women were as handy as most men. They would saw, cut wood, and help in building sheds. Some of these operations would cause accidents, and if not too serious, they were treated at home.

In the early days, one could depend upon doctors' visitations: here they come with their little black handbags, a prayer, and the horse-driven chaise. During these visits, the doctor instructed the parents how to handle various emergencies such as choking, fainting, head lice, and bleeding wounds. Children were always concerned about doctors, so they had to improvise. They would let the children put the stethoscope on their dolls. A few trinkets would suffice to calm them down. A common question by children was, "Did you have your appendix removed? Well, are you lucky." Ambulances were scarce, so one got to the hospital as best he could. Many of the doctors traveled through bad weather, knowing that the family was terribly frightened. God bless all of them.

Midwives were a wonderful group of people. Hard working, low fees—if any; consider the expenses, then and now. Can you imagine the American Indian, riding down the trail with her husband? She tells him to stop, she dismounts from her horse, walks into the woods, has her baby, mounts her horse with the baby, and all three ride into the sunset.

Fear of dentists was quite common among children as it was with the adults. As you sat there, the pain seemed to go away. If a child had a loose tooth, there were scientific methods applied. First you shake the loose tooth, next you tie a string around it and then to the door knob. Now, gently close the door and voilá—gone! Some old codgers, odd fellows, could apply a pair of pliers to the tooth and give it a yank.

The best part of the tooth-pulling was that the victim was rewarded twice, once by the parents and once by the "tooth fairy." For the tooth fairy you had to place the tooth under your pillow, and the following morning there was the reward. Some people had a gold tooth, which was a sign of nobility. It seemed to create a perpetual smile.

For us kids, it was not necessary to see a barber unless you had a growth on your head. These old time barbers could first-aid your head; they could get rid of cuts, cut skin, and carbuncles. The older people went to the barber but not the children. The expression "going to pot" was based upon the fact that the parents put a pot upon the kid's head and cut around it—a real barbarity.

Our modes of transportation in Garfield were horse and wagon, bicycles, roller skates, and, later on, buses. The horse and wagon was improved for transportation, the wagon fitted with round seats for people to sit on and travel from city to city. Deliveries were made by electric cars called "pie wagons," which were fitted with solid rubber tires. Later, the police used these cars, converted with a rear door and all the latest gadgets, to transport the drunks to the clink.

Later came the trolley cars, but they did not travel too far.

Around the year 1924, at the tender age of nine, I clearly remember the old time buses which had a sign posted on the insides, reading

> *Step back and give others a chance*
> *Do not smoke or spit*
> *Or you might be under arrest*

The roads were something to live with: water puddles, dirt, and dust. We must remember there were no streets or sidewalks, no telephone poles, no electricity. One could see some frightened horses run down the road with the entire wagon. Cats and dogs had the "run of the mill." Dogs ran rampant, no control, and the dog population increased. Cats, given no respect, were often chased away from homes. There were very few vets in the vicinity to aid these animals. The food was mostly scraps from the table. When they became sick, we could only surmise the cause or cure. Both animals multiplied by the hundreds, with not much care for either. Some men, while walking their dogs, would challenge another man's dog to a fight. Our dog was very large, and he won every battle.

Horses were of great value. They were protected because there were numerous jobs for them.

These horses were used to transport people as well as dig cellars for new homes.

Most men and women had various trades, because in their home country it was required by law. My father's training was tailoring, but the only tailoring he did was make us all our clothes. (Sometimes my breath came in short pants.) Here, again, was togetherness. Neighbors helped each other, thus saving the cost of commercial material.

As kids, when we were able to read, the Herald newspaper became an integral part of our lives. We admired the funnies, like Buffalo Bill and Pop Wortle, the string saver (this grew into a giant ball of immense proportions). Then there was the "terrible Mr. Bang" and a little girl illustrated holding a handkerchief to her little sister's nose, saying, "Now, blow.'" We had Bunkey Hill, Jr., who said "I wish my dear mother were here to protect me." There are still a few old timers to remember these antics. Each day, another illustration appeared, a completely black square, and underneath it was written "And so far into the night." It was years later that I realized what it meant. Other uses for the newspaper were insulation, stuffing holes in outhouses, sheds, and barns, singeing the hair off pigs, and also making sailor hats and sailboats.

During the winter, small ponds froze. We could not afford ice skates or skis, but we did have Yankee ingenuity. Our first encounter with the icy pond was to back off a few yards, run like heck, and slide over the ice. Some kid who had skates would lend them to us for a while. Sometimes if we found only one skate, we would still have fun, thus the origin of "cheap skate." We formulated our own skis. We broke up an old barrel, pulled out the staves, mounted some fixtures, adjusted it to our foot, and there you are. Now, everyone, stand back—here we come down the steep hill.

The outhouse was usually located in the back of the house, on an area where the overflow would not contaminate the grounds. Also, it must always be kept a good distance from the well. The Australians called their expansive land the "outback." Though not too romantic, many of the girls solved their problems while sitting on a double receptacle. I could never conceive of sitting next to another person testing for deodorants.

The doors on most of these outhouses contained a half-moon logo. I don't know the meaning—I never stayed long enough to figure it out. The large catalogs were used in the outhouses. Care was taken not to use the pages with the farm implements. This method was great for advertising.

After many deposits into the base of the outhouse, it was time to remove or cover the ingredients. In came the neighbors, the new hole was dug, and the outhouse was then relocated. No picnic, no singing, just contentment. Now we could say, "My cup does not runneth over." As Churchill said, "It was too little and too late."

In these very old days, there were no benefits, social security, welfare, or unemployment payments. We had an insurance agent who collected five to twenty cents and up weekly. The payment for losing a leg or an arm was only a very small amount, because the people could not afford much.

Due to large families, it became inevitable that families required the hand-me-downs syndrome. This was created by additional children who grew out of their clothes. Local families participated in giving other families their outgrown clothes. We could also call this "Passover."

We all had to pitch in, in order to make all things work. Just a few reminders: make beds, clean the house, do the dishes (no dishwasher), cut and store firewood, help in the garden (this was very important, all the material was put in jars for the winter). Feed the animals, go shopping, service the kerosene lamps, make beds, take a rest and try again. Whew.

But there were advantages, like no fuses to blow, no leaky pipes, no jammed toilets, no sewer lines to clog, no dryer or dishwasher to break down, no telephone lines, no telephones. Thank goodness there were hardly any costs. Families had all the animals to keep the wolf from the door.

Our landlord was Valentine Barney, who we nicknamed Barney Google:

> *Barney Google, with those googly, googly eyes*
> *Barney Google, had a wife three times his size*
> *When his horses ran that day*
> *Barney ran the other way*
> *Barney Google, with those googly, googly eyes*

Barney wanted me to take a trip to his farm around Allwood Road in Clifton (back in the old days there were many farms.) Since I was just a kid, he asked my mother if I could go with him. First we loaded the wagon. He helped me climb to the driver's seat. I sat there very proudly, all attentive. What am I supposed to do next? I wondered. He handed me the reins and told me to hold them very firmly. Looking back now, I imagine how I must have felt: like an astronaut going to the moon, or like someone climbing Mt. Everest, or like a diver finding a ship that had sunk with all its treasures.

Barney consoled me, patted me on my back, and said, "Give a slight tug on the reins and tell the horse 'gid-yap'." At first the horse started slowly, then gained greater speeds. Faster, faster he went; now he became a horse with the speed of light. Telephone poles appeared like hedges, as a cloud of dust rose alongside us. After an unaccounted time we arrived at our destination. I was utterly exhausted—and secretly relieved

There were no telephone poles, the horse traveled about ten miles an hour, no pit stops, the entire trip from Garfield was about ten miles. "Ode to a toad."

The base of the average home had a dug-out cellar. It is very interesting to compare the construction methods with today's excavations. Bulldozers, cranes—no way. It started with the horse and an attached scoop, which when drawn by the horse would pick up the surface as the horse continued to circle the projected area. The horse with the scoop would remove the soil, place it on one side of the excavation, and continue until it could not convey any soil because of the angle it had to haul the soil up from then on. A crew of men with shovels would remove the remaining soil, no horsin' around.

Because of heavy rains, many cellars become flooded. As a kid, I saw some cellars that were flooded as much as three feet. Some of the tenants put their valuables in a raft or small boat to save the items. How did they remove the water? There was a long pipe, about ten feet long, and about six or more inches wide. At one end was a double handle where two men could draw the water from the cellar, the other end was inserted into the cellar's flooded area, and away they pumped. I still have just that type of pump, and visitors and friends are amazed to note that the pump is at least one hundred years old.

School Daze

I went to school in 1920, at the age of five. It was #5 school on Outwater Lane in Garfield, N.J. Although we had a sufficient amount of discipline at home, we objected to the type of discipline at school.

My first day at school was hazardous to my health. The teacher sat me down at a table with the other kids, who were playing with blocks and dolls. She assumed I would enjoy this part of the training, to which I strenuously objected. This was not my soda or whatever she was serving. The next ordeal was that she had the boys on one side and girls on the other side facing each other. While at this silly stance, we had to sing "How do you do my partner, how do you do today? We will dance in a circle. I will show you the way." No way. I had no use for girls to begin with. At home we ignored them, kids who associated with girls were sissies. She gave up and noted that I was incorrigible. In those days the teachers had full power, like the queens of old. Thank goodness none of us were ever beheaded.

As I grew older, my troubles escalated. We kids, naturally, enjoyed chewing all sorts of things. However, gum chewing was my downfall. Oh yes, we were adept at chewing bubble gum. All teachers had sight like a hawk in full swing after its prey. This one observed me chewing a mile a minute. Lines of apprehension appeared on my suntanned face. Contact was made. Ah-ha! She called me to the desk and with a talented sneer advised me of my rights and if I could not afford a lawyer I could have the principal. The further instructions were, "Now remove that substance from your foul mouth, place it on your nose, and leave it there until the cows come home."

I got one of my science books and found just what I was looking for: an eye for an eye. With great enthusiasm, I went to the candy store next to the school and purchased a material that you could chew. It had a sweet substance, and was great because, although it appeared like gum, it would not stick on my nose under these trying conditions.

The next day, I again sat in my chair, with complete confidence. Then, uh-oh—the teacher spotted me from her control tower, and she beckoned me to approach the landing field. "Well, my good man, what has thou of interest for me today?" That was pretty stupid; she knew darn well I was chewing gum. She started her well-trained procedures on command: place the gum on your nose, stand in front of the class, and present yourself as a stupid imbecile. With a sly grin, I knew she did not realize that she was accosting one of the young intellectuals, the "Master." Then, with a hideous grin, she said, "Place the gum on your nose." The moment of truth. "Dear Teacher, 'tis not gum that I was chewing, it is a wax composition that will not adhere to anything." "Ah so," she said. "Let's make a scientific experiment. Take the darn thing, put a curve in it, and place it over your nose, and hold your head up so that it will not fall off." Dearly beloved, my chewing days were over "toot-sweet."

Some of you old timers will get a kick out of remembering the young entrepreneurs who at the age of twelve were always seeking their fortune. There was an advertisement about selling a salve called "Rose-Bud Salve." This was used for cuts and bruises. The cost per container was 25 cents, and it had the appearance of a shoe-shine can. If you sold a certain amount, you would receive a gift. I sold enough to earn a telescope, two and a half feet long. After checking on the neighborhood's "aura," I knew that I was no dope cause I had the scope. This was to me a great treasure, and I would take it wherever I would go. Who knows, I might be called on to explain the celestial and heavenly bodies.

One day will live in infamy. I went to school with my telescope, climbed up on the windowsill, and scanned the heavenly orbits of the vast universe. All of a sudden, a fiendish hand reached out behind my neck and yanked me off the pedestal. It was none other than another teacher with physical prowess. A lecture, beyond human comprehension. She wrestled my telescope from my hands and said I would get it back at the end of the school term. I returned to my seat with an aura of disobedience. She will rue the day, I thought. She did not realize that my studies could culminate in a great study of the universe called "Celestial Phenomena." She had yet to discover that a kid of twelve could be so determined and dominant in his beliefs.

I worked very hard to earn the telescope, and I was going to prove that nothing could obliterate my intense attitude of science. Now the tide turneth. During that school term, I did not pay attention to any lecture or class participation. The proof of the pudding was that I was the only one in the entire school to receive a "minus zero" in my grades. The teacher was fortunate she did not report her findings to my father. He would have told her off, #@**% and four tenths. Suffer not ye little brats.

Regarding school days, it was a dangerous time for all of us kids. We gathered around the school grounds, where the "ring leaders" were active, and the lower echelon were following the roles of their leaders. Remember the spinning top? This unit consisted of winding a string around the top and pulling it, then letting go and the top would spin on the ground. Along came our fearless leaders (the creeps) and asked if we had a hole drilled into the top. If not, they would take away our tops. Sounds like the government. A day at a time.

Another gag was to have our leaders place a stick on our shoulders and stand back. This was to create a fight. With that, they would then say, "Three-six-nine, the fight is mine, I'll fight you any old time." This unholy tradition was terminated when my cousin, a large, strapping fellow who was in the Golden Gloves, intervened. Power is strength.

One day I was sitting in my classroom chair while a full-blown test was going on. Inadvertently, my eyes roamed around, across the aisle, to catch a few correct answers. Hearing footsteps behind me, I straightened up. I finally realized that this loving teacher was sneaking up on me. The teacher put a hand on each side of my head and slammed both hands together. This created an astounding clap of thunder. It was fortunate that the hands were not on my ears. I thought the Walls of Jericho had come tumbling down. This gesture could have created a hearing loss.

There are more stories from the torture chamber. If we, for some reason, went astray, we would have to hold out our hands, palms up, and the teacher would give us a few whacks with a ruler. Luckily, it was not a foot. If for some reason you went to the principal, he would ask you to bend over, and he applied a few paddles. And you would have to bend over, even if you name wasn't Ben Dover.

For the non-intellectuals, there was a pointed hat called the "dunce cap." This was presented to you and you sat in the fifth row, last seat. Another old trick was dipping the girls' hair in the ink well. For shame. If the school informed our patents of our misconduct, we would also be punished. Try these adventures for our misguided brats of today. It did not take too long to see "Edison" (that is, the light).

A good procedure was to require every student to read aloud in front of the class some items presented by the teacher. For example, mine was "Fish Builds Brains." Well, I confronted the teacher, telling her and the class that I read an article in the paper that contested that statement, saying it was "not conclusive." She said, "Sit down." In another "sit down session" I read that the pirates were on an island. I told the teacher that the spelling was wrong, the "s" should be removed. Again the cry, "Sit down!" Another note to read was "Wind is air in motion," however there was no "Sit down!" I thought—it is better to air, but do it alone.

Back in 1920, mom used to say, "Bank the fire, turn down the kerosene lamp, fluff up the feather bed, and scoot off to bed." Adventure in the days of your, mine, or his.

The Sharp Razor: A True Story

Although none of us kids liked to get hair cuts, we still had to graduate from the old days when they put the preverbal pot on our heads to round a guy out. With the new style hair cuts it was really better, because now the other kids did not say that we were going to pot.

Today was a normal day, but not for the barber. Today he decided to become a runner and dashed down the street with his strap hanging in mid-air. The people who knew him noticed that something was wrong, so they called the gendarmes, who naturally captured him and put him into the pie-wagon.

Forsooth, so what was a pie-wagon? The pie-wagon was a sort of truck that was a police wagon, which had a large back door and railings. This was instrumental in taking the drunks and the unruly to jail. At least the police and their fledglings went to Scotland Yard in style (not really).

Night followed day, and upon some scientific research we learned that our hair stylist was incarcerated by Garfield's finest (this incident occurred in New Jersey, planet Earth).

His entrapment was brief. Due to his fine attitude in close quarters, they finally released him.

But this was the pull that rang the bell. The poor soul placed a sign in the barber shop window, which read, "I am OK now."

This situation was unreal. How could we sit in the chair while the razor was hovering above our heads. It reminded me of the king who had the sword hanging over his head.

This is a true story, and we were really sad to think that we lost our friend who always encouraged us and always was there when we needed some advice.

'Tis the cutting edge.

Judges and Gangsters

Imagine yourself sitting on the judge's bench and having to pass sentence on the surge of intellectuals who are never guilty. A plaintiff complained that a fellow stole some bottles of beer from him. The judge pondered for a moment and asked the number of beer bottles that the alleged criminal stole. With malice towards none, the man said about 15 bottles. "Well, my good man, 15 bottles of beer do not make a case." Case closed.

Then there was the fellow who the judge said to please approach the bench. Well, all hell broke loose when the fellow brought up a stool. Yes, the judge recovered.

Speaking of bootleggers, the reason they called them that was that they hid the booze bottles in their boots. When the cops noticed the fellow walking in a funny manner, they said "Boot up." No puss in boots.

Although the gangsters have almost disappeared, there are many intruders of all types— pickpockets, car-jackers, break-in and rape artists of all kinds. How about the car jackers—why don't we hang them as they did for stealing a horse? Boy, that would stop it immediately.

Just watch the women in the shopping centers. They leave their bags in the carriages and continue shopping. To produce a "grand awakening" I tell them that they have a nice looking pocketbook. Lazy Mary, will you get up.

During the days of yore, or mob rule, as kids on our way to school all of a sudden we heard some rapid shots from a gun. In fact, it was a machine gun. There on one of the buildings was a man running for his life from roof to roof, while below was a gangster with a machine gun rapidly firing in an attempt to obliterate this pour soul. Yes, he got away, that time. Although gangsters were not masons, after the slaughter they put the victim's feet in a bucket of cement. Good for balance, and when they threw them into the Passaic River they swayed to and fro, while the fish swam by.

Some of the local citizens were quite ingenious. They had their stills in the basements, and above the roofs you could see some smoke emerging from the pigeon coops. In another means to conceal their precious stills, they dug tunnels under the house to ship out the products. Some of us kids did a good deed for our fathers. We went shopping in the fruit markets, where they gave us our bag of fruit and then bagged the pint bottle of booze. I suppose here we can call it "Fruit-Up." As one romantic bootlegger said to the girl, "I love your still."

We had a secret code or knock. If you wanted to enter the gin mill (saloon), you just knocked twice and asked for Gus. When our fathers were late coming home after work, we went to the gin mill and opened the swinging doors and yelled, "Is my father there?"

This was the "den of iniquity." Every gin mill supported a spittoon. This was a handsome receptacle placed on the floor at the foot of the bar, within range of the expectorant (plain spit). Those bar flies were like FBI men, straight shooters. It sounded like "ping." Ugh. On the men's room wall was a sign, "We aim to please, hope your aim is good."

On the border of East Paterson and Garfield existed a playground which was used for all types of sports. A short distance away was a hill called Cherry Hill. This area contained the proper sand for us kids to play with our trains, cars, and many other toys. On a clear and beautiful day, while thus playing, we heard the sound of a powerful car pulling up to the top of the hill. It contained Garfield's finest group of indigents, just peering at us and waving howdy. We waved back, and then they jumped out of their touring cars. Equipped with hand and machine guns, they just kept firing away, got back into their cars, waved bye, and rode off into the sunset. Wow. Here you see that these gangsters were in charge of the town. On occasion one could see while riding down Market Street a few good bodies lying along the road. Dead men tell no tales. Next time you get a hair cut, get a "crime wave."

The gang war was prevalent throughout the land. My brother had a green car, and as he stepped into the barber shop, he heard a gunshot and went out to see the reason. He found a bullet hole in his fender. They thought he was the enemy. After hearing that, I purchased a blue car. This episode took place around 1927. Nice time. As one guy said, cansumption be done about it (Uh-cough, uh- cough).

Many alcoholics died from tainted liquor. I believe that a good brain is a terrible thing to waste. That's if you have one. Now I smoke bacon and ham. I also drink orange juice.

How to Bug Your Neighbors

Kids' stuff, but fun. As kids, we lived in a group of homes numbering about thirty. Here we had a baseball field and other types of sports areas to exercise our pent-up emotions.

In a place of this sort, there was always a neighbor, or shall we say "Mad Hatter," who yelled, Get off the lawn, Don't cut through our yard, Keep your dog away from our property, endlessly. We used ingenious methods to get even.

Here is the first fiendish method, "The Bugs." Take an old tire tube and cut a small piece off, about three inches square. Place a screw through the middle, then tie a long string to the screw, so that you can be at a distance when the fun begins.

Now spit on the piece of tube and place it on the window. Believe me, it will stick. At the other end of the string, make about ten knots. Now run your fingers along the knots, and this will cause a vibration on the window, so the victim will hear it and come out. Suggestion: if you are doing this in the winter with snow on the ground, us a white string. By the same token, use a green string in the summer.

What will happen? Well, the occupants of the stricken house will parade around the outside of the house and shake their heads in great confusion. For shame. Oh, before I forget, after you pull the string and notice some commotion on the inside of the house, yank the string and the tire cut will fall to the ground. This could be repeated because we at that time did not have 911.

We did not wait for Halloween, it was too far away. We forged ahead, like the blacksmith.

"Grass, trap, and ouch." Ingredients: use a small mouse-like trap, so as not to cause too much pain. Remember, we did not want to bury our neighbors but to hassle them. We had our right to remain silent, but did not succumb. So let's get on with it.

First select your victim, place the trap on the back porch, and sprinkle some fresh grass over the trap, just enough not to overplay the game. Now you must devise some method to alert the poor soul. Shhhhh, here he comes. He approaches the trap and gives it a good kick. Wham! The trap ensnares his big toe. It is these moments that make history and should be written in the archives to perpetuate the next generations of misfits.

"The bell ringers." The equipment required is very simple. Take a straight pin and approach the front door of the "ringed." Slip the needle into the bell button, just inside the unit. Now stand back for a moment. Isn't this the "peace resistance"? I ask you. Just watch, the householder assumes that a visitor has arrived, only to find the pin in the bell-stack.

You can say that you have corrupted the bats in the belfry.

This is a far cry in the wilderness when we compare today's brazen antics, which are beyond comprehension. So take the lumps.

My father was an early astronaut. Even as a boy, I learned all about space. Father said, One foot for mankind, and the other for my son.

Let's ask the kids of today if they would tolerate these old-day methods:

1. If you were caught smoking, father would say, Now chew it. He was very considerate, and would stand by until you stopped vomiting.

2. Before the magic age of 18, and even when 18, he would receive you with the "cat of nine tails" if you came home late. The cat would be waiting for you. The cat was a stick equipped with nine strings of leather strips. Ca-peesh?

3. Mother always said, if you got out of line, Wait till your father comes home; or, Finish the job your father assigned to you, or else Pow!

4. I never had any gum trouble. When lying, you were treated to various detergents. (May I hold your palm, Olive? Not on your life, boy.)

5. Standing in the corner while cooling off, if you missed this.

Today my brother Lou, a retired minister, muses about the time he was a young lad and someone said that he was not fit to sleep with pigs.

On occasion, my uncle would visit us on his motorcycle. We really enjoyed these visits, because in the old days, when travel required time and distance to see loved ones, our appreciation was untold.

Ill fated, my uncle told my brother that if anything happened to him, Lou should keep all the tools he had. Eventually, the sad day came to pass. On one of these trips to visit us he had an accident with his motorcycle and died on the spot. All his tools were now brother Lou's possessions. What to do with all the tools? He gave all of them to a very good family friend, who showed his appreciation by presenting Lou with a young piglet. Lou adored this pig, and made my mother laugh when he tied a ribbon around its neck and paraded it around the house.

One day my father left word that Lou must clean the headquarters of his pig, which was now full grown. When Dad, Pop, or "The Master" said jump, you did not come down until the orders were given to descend. Not like today, when mother says, "This is the last time I tell you." There never was a last time for the five of us kids. Lou did not need a lecture to thus perform. With latitude and longitude, our hero began the arduous task of pig-o-nometry.

Hi ho, hi ho, off to the pigpen we go, semi-laughing all the way. This was no ordinary pigpen. It had a clean outer floor made of cement, and also consisted of a large bin which was well laden with straw. Lou cleaned the interior and supplied it with fresh straw. Well, he said, this is a job well done by your treasury agents. Ho-hum, a little tired, he went into the pen and fell sound asleep.

Finally, he awoke with the call from my mother, Hey Lou, hey Lou. When he awoke, he noticed the pig sleeping next to him. With a jubilant cry he said in a little voice just above a whisper, "Now when people tell me that I am not fit to sleep with the pigs, this will prove that I am." A large smile predominates his countenance when he recalls this incident. That little pig did not go to market.

Around 1910, many families had various groups of animals. As kids, we raised snakes, rabbits, frogs, cats, dogs, you name it. We always had something to do, we did not need all the modern paraphernalia of modern day addicts. At this time, I believed in the rabbits foot, but lost interest when I discovered its origin. With our vast collection of snakes and other things, here was the time to study the real metamorphosis or transformation of these creatures. We at times had a display and charged the kids five cents to witness the archeological finds. Then we went to the carnival, where there was a crier who yelled, "Step right up, folks, and see Myola, the strange and curious creature, alive, walks, talks, and eats like an animal. Come young and old, for one tenth of a dollar, step right up."

I almost became a pigeon fancier. One of the boys who had some birds interested me in a bird he wanted to see. I purchased it when he said was a full-blooded homer. The cost was one dollar. He said the bird could win races. A homer is a bird that is used for competitive racing. The idea is to release the birds hundreds of miles from home, and the one that comes in first is the winner. Each bird has a tiny key attached to its foot. When the bird checks in, the owner takes the key and inserts it into a machine that will register the time of entry. Shattered nerves, for I took this bird about two miles from home and it arrived back in "no time," which was two days, nothing fancier. Those were the daze.

The Forstmann Woolen Co.

Botany Worsted Mills, Passaic, N.J.

The Forstmann Woolen Company also included the Botany Mills in Passaic, N.J. They were instrumental in the betterment of the lives of thousands of people. Although none of our family worked in the Botany Co., we at times shared their problems. This company was employing many people who depended on their livelihood, especially after coming to America.

The Botany Worsted Mill was built in 1890, and the Forstmann Woolen Mills was built in 1902. They both settled in this area because of the city's abundant water supply, between the Passaic River and the Dundee Canal, and its proximity to New York.

Passaic industry developed later than most cities', when the immigration pattern had switched from mostly Irish and English immigrants to southern and eastern Europeans. The Slovak people joined the development of the city, and immigrants from Poland sent word back home that work was abundant. In the 1890s, Jews came from small towns in eastern Europe, where czarist dictators allowed them to live only in certain areas of the town.

By 1910, Passaic had become known as the "City of Immigrants," and by 1920, the Polish population totaled 17,000. Other nationalities included Ukrainians and Italians, but the largest group was from Austrian Galicia.

At the peak of production in 1918, 10,000 out of 21,000 workers in Passaic worked in the Botany and Forstmann plants. David Goldberg wrote about immigration labor at the turn of the century in his book called *A Tale of Three Cities,* namely Passaic, Clifton, and Garfield. "Work at the plants, where raw wool was processed into finished cloth, was long and oppressive. The raw wool was foul smelling and greasy, and workers often contacted anthrax, which came to be known as the 'wool-sorter's disease'."

Women made up half of the work force in the plants, because the jobs did not require heavy lifting. Women split their time between raising families and working at the factory, working a special 8 p.m. to 6 a.m. shift.

A series of strikes in 1912 was followed by a year of long strikes by 20,000 workers, which paralyzed factories in Garfield, Clifton, and East Paterson.

Workers struck in 1926 because Botany and Forstmann had cut their pay and to protest long hours and poor working conditions. There was not much time for workers to be involved in anything other than raising a family and working long hours, and community life centered around the Catholic church.

The Forstmann Woolen Company had built about 30 company homes in Garfield, N.J., off Lanza Avenue. Only plant workers were permitted to rent these homes.

My two brothers and sister were employed at Forstmann in Garfield. I started at this plant in 1933, at the age of 18, as a machine oilier, keeping the machines at top running speeds. Between jobs, I was required to run errands for the office. If my hands were still oily, I took a paper and covered the mail. Lift that bail, tote that barge.

On one of these trips to the office, one of the main office managers asked me a question about something that he was interested in. I told him that I did not know the answer. With a stern voice, he told me that an apprentice should know many of these questions. He was taken aback when I told him that I was not an apprentice, and he said that I appeared to be a hard-working young man, and should enter the company's apprentice program. He told me to follow him to the plant manager's office. He introduced me to a man who asked me if I would be interested. I thanked him and wondered if I would get permission from my mother. He said that he had never head of a thing like that, but laughed and joked that if my mother approved, I could start on Monday. Incidentally, there was a long list in waiting for this apprentice program. (Before I get into trouble, I must mention my sister Mathilda, or Mitzie, and thank her for getting me the job in the first place.)

The apprentice program was a three-year term. The program was set up to make a six-month period in each of the woolen mill areas, then make an extra two years in the laboratory. Of the six months in each department, the fifth month was under the supervision of the boss. After the entire program, I was assigned to the wool spinning department. The training in the laboratory enabled me to understand all the types of materials used in the manufacture of wool.

By this time, the war was on and I enlisted in the Army Signal Corps and served my basic training at Camp Crowder, Mo.

When I returned from the war in Europe, my company manager introduced me to the president of the entire two plants of the Forstmann Woolen

Company. The plant manager, my boss, mentioned that he would like to assign me to his staff and be a liaison between his department managers and himself.

The washhouse department was unique in its operation. The first step was to sort the wool into various phases, which was done by the wool sorters. My brother Louis was a supervisor there. The raw wool was then sent to the wool spinning department where it was washed and sent into a dryer. From there it went to the wool mixing department, where a mixture was made to the right color and quality. The wool was then sent to the carding department. Here the wool was sent through a series of rollers containing short wires on rolls which rotated around a large cylinder, and then finished by several flat rollers and wound onto rolls, which were then taken to the wool spinning department.

The raw wool was introduced into the hopper, which emptied into long rectangular vats. These vats, in series, contained from 1500 to 2000 gallons. Wool cannot be pushed along by water pressure; instead it was moved by tines like the points of a fork. These tines moved in a long rectangular motion, which propelled the wool forward as it traveled to the next squeeze rollers. In the large vats was soap and soda to wash the wool While the soap did a good job, when there was a breakdown and the machine had to be stopped the soda would harm the wool. This system had been in place for about 50 years.

Not long after I was assigned to this department as quality control, and supervised all the wool, I spoke to the head of our laboratory, Mr. Wolf. A chemist in our lab investigated, and after various tests formulated a plan to use another type of detergent, without soda, and by golly, there was no more problem. The machine breakdown could wait. Unlike soda, which after washing left he wool flat, the new detergent puffed up the wool and permitted it to dry faster, thus the increasing production three-fold.

All the plant's textile machinery came from Germany. Ten of our old carding machines became obsolete and the plant manager decided to purchase ten new carding machines for $800,000 from the Newport News shipyard. At that time they were building the *S.S. United States.* With two of my foremen, I visited the plant to investigate the progress. Well, sir, we were wined and dined by the president of that company for about a week. Since I was a supervisor of quality control, I planned the meetings at our plant with their supers and engineers to set up a so-called "shakedown cruise."

At Forstmann, I also set up the training program for new apprentices, who were required to complete a high school diploma and had to be eighteen years of age. I supervised their three year apprentice training. In fact, I was instrumental in designing the course.

When I noticed that some of these young men were top grade, I suggested that they look for other promising position. At least one went to West Point. When the course was completed after three years, their graduation was held at the Forstmann Library in Passaic.

The Forstmann Woolen Co. consisted of three main departments, the Garfield Woolen Division, the Weaving Department, and the Passaic Finishing Plant. My position as a quality control supervisor required me to ensure that he three divisions were up to standard in manufacturing the proper material for production.

Why did the textile mills close down? In the older days, you needed the warmth of woolen clothing, especially standing out in freezing weather waiting for a bus or walking to work. Later, with the advent of better transportation like buses and cars, the heavy clothing was not required.

After fifty years, the famous Forstmann Woolen Company, as well as Botany, finally closed its doors. You can imagine the thousands of people who were out of a job. My career was "ka-put." As president Roosevelt said, this was a day of infamy. I was only one of the few that remained at the plant when Stevens bought out our mill. I flew with some officials to various textile companies to try to revive our company, but no luck. After six months with Stevens, I tried to find other jobs. They said I was overqualified and so that was the end of the story. I later went into the painting business.

Get the Lead Out

In the good old days, lead paint was used on the interior and exterior of many buildings. All went well until the complaints by many parents that children were chewing and eating the lead paint from the window sills, as well as lead paint dust from doors and floors. Some of the children were affected by this exposure. (Painters were required to mix the lead paint by hand, a laborious task. The exposure also affected many painters who had been exposed to lead-paint for many years.) Lead paint had existed for years in homes and commercial buildings, but very few people realized that this hazardous condition existed. The eastern area--New Jersey, New York Pennsylvania--was more involved. A drastic method was required to create a safer haven for the affected children.

Parents were devastated and now wanted the government to take action immediately. All lead-paint manufactures were notified to immediately stop producing the lead-paint, as well as having this paint removed from the store shelves (pronto). We needed to overhaul the entire system, and we needed to do this nationwide.

Washington suggested that all lead paint manufacturers "get on it" right away, that they should formulate a plan and submit it as soon as possible. As a house painter, I had the opportunity to learn about this condition, although I did not paint with lead paint.

At a meeting of paint manufacturers, the speaker asked all attending that were involved in this program to submit their analysis, so that they could go on and come to a decision on the right steps to be taken and finally present Washington with the right solution. The group was at a loss to solve this momentous problem that was causing a nationwide calamity.

One speaker mentioned that his father, who had spent most of his life in the paint programs, could not attend because of an illness. But after a dark cloud, some rain, and perhaps a dash of snow, there finally was that proverbial silver lining. The speaker raised his hands and asked for complete silence. All were apprehensive, what could the speaker have to solve this problem?

All attention was now directed to the podium. The speaker, now all enthused, smiled, and said, "I just remembered what my father said." The group was on the edge of their chairs.

"Son, get the lead out."

A Smart Priest

When I was about twelve, The Forstmann Co. had some thirty homes built, where we kids had a ball. There was a ball field and in back of the property was a swamp that had about a foot of water when it rained. Here we played with a makeshift wooden boat that lasted about an hour before flooding. We stood out of the water, turned over the boat, and sailed on in style.

We had a gang, all around twelve years of age, better known as the gathering of the brains. 'Twas like a football huddle. Here great decisions were made. Little Joey Feist told us about the interesting event that had transpired at his class in the Catholic church school. A nun in his class prepared the students for the proper protocol when a priest visited to review the class. He would be certain to ask some questions about our surrounding world.

The father entered the room and all the students stood up and were quite tense. He asked the first question: Who created the heavens? Came the answer, "God, God, God." Very good, a splendid answer. Next, "Who created our world?" Again, "God, God, God." Smart answer. The last question was, "Who built this church?" Our hero Joey said, in a shaky voice just above a whisper, "The carpenters."

The class was dumbfounded; they were sure Joey would be excommunicated. But to their continued shock, the priest went over to Joey and placed his hands on the boy's head. "My true and faithful servant, you exemplified the true nature of our Christian Catholic beliefs." The nun was amazed.

This reminds me of the fellow who wrote the dictionary. When his wife came home and caught him kissing the maid, she said, "I'm surprised." He then corrected her by saying, "You were amazed, I was surprised."

At our next meeting of the "think tank," Joey explained that, since the class was still confused, he did not know whether he would ever recover from that onslaught. So be it. Amen, and glory be to God.

The Pope Slept Here

Eventually, in his travels to many countries conveying good deeds and good will, I am sure Pope John Paul II remembers the time he spent at the ranch house in Clifton, the home of Dr. Philipzack. I speak of this proudly, because this is the house that I built.

To make this story a little more interesting, let me relate the entire process from purchasing a lot from Myron T. Holman, Sr., who is now president of the Shotmeyer Oil Co. That was the beginning of the Cardinal's jet take off to Rome, where he became the great Pope of Rome and a saint beloved by the entire world. Before I jettison the jet to Rome, I will relate the interesting drama of this story.

Since the street called Fenlon Boulevard was a "paper street," after purchasing the property I inquired regarding the existence of a sewer line. It did exist, and the next move was to clear all the unnecessary shrubs and debris from the entrance at Passaic Avenue. With the city's permission, my brother-in-law, Ted Gambuti, cut a temporary road several hundred feet long to access the area in which I would build the ranch house. Incidentally, the sewer line had not been used. When I found it under several inches and after removing the sewer cover there was only some sand, indicating that it was never used and free of any sediment. Ted also put a sewer line to the ranch house. Then began breathtaking hard work for more than a year, because I built almost all of the house by myself, with minimal help. The entire three sides of the house were built with cinder blocks, but the front was brick and wood. The electrical work, plumbing, and heating were done by professionals. The bank loan required that I own the property, and required several stages of building to complete the loan.

I was a quality control supervisor at the Forstmann Woolen Company of Garfield, N.J. It was after work that I was able to work on the ranch house. Years later I sold the ranch house to Dr. Philipzak. (I next built a split-level house next to the ranch house. However, I also sold this house and moved to a nearby area.)

To continue this romantic episode, Dr. Philipzak's wife was an opera singer with a beautiful voice that could be heard throughout the neighborhood. More research revealed that his wife was also the cardinal's niece. The cardinal enjoyed visiting with the Philipzaks. He could be seen swimming in their backyard pool. On occasion, the media would take pictures of the cardinal and publish or televise them

The cardinal never rested. His mystic powers were relegated to any area where he could exercise his good will and blessings. On one of his walks in the neighborhood, he came upon a man busy on his property, hard at work removing some heavy rocks. "My good man," he said, "it is very admirable to do hard work, but life is too short to work so hard." Joe was astounded, and promised to mend his ways. The cardinal then blessed Joe and went on his way.

We are very happy to see that the pope went to Cuba, and left an aura of great significance. The Cuban people were ecstatic and long will remember this outstanding visit. Human rights activists say that Cuba is releasing some of the political prisoners on the list submitted by the Vatican during Pope John Paul's visit. A real historic epic. It is of great interest to view him on TV and follow his great contributions to the world. May Pope John Paul II live forever in body and soul.

Religion

The World Book Encyclopedia says that religion is "man's acceptance of the existence of supreme and superhuman powers, usually inherent in beings or gods who are worshipped by the believers. Systems ordinarily acquire ceremonial rites and practices which are strictly adhered to."

Too much has been written about religion to collect or summarize, but I believe that the Ten Commandments would suffice for a start. Amen.

"The Sawdust Trail" was the name for the old time religious tent meetings, usually held outdoors. On the floor was strewn some sawdust. These tents accommodated a large number of people. There were no loudspeakers, so the pastor usually had an operatic voice.

The good preacher would walk up and down the aisle, gesturing and looking for lost souls. He often mentioned that if we did not reform, we would go straight to hell. Most people who entered the tent had never encountered such a show.

While the gathering would sing a hymn, the preacher beckoned the sinners to walk up the sawdust trail and meet the Lord and be saved. Quite a few came up the trail, and when leaving, they were overjoyed to have been saved. Amen.

When we speak of Billy Graham, and read or watch him on TV or other media messages, we know that he has a word for not only us but for the rest of the world. For those who do not have religious beliefs, there is something to attain to renew their beliefs. He does not want people to stand with a group on top of a hill and be lifted into the heavens to the distant land called heaven.

And don't forget the Salvation Army—good as it can be. They give their services in all disasters. Give a little, receive a lot.

As a scoutmaster for some 60 years and still active, I noticed that any boy from a church background was easier to deal with. They were always more attentive than the rest of the group. They learned the lessons more quickly.

And devout people live longer, too. Research shows that people who go to church are healthier than those who don't. Researchers took blood samples from 1,700 senior citizens and asked them about their church attendance. People who went to church at least once a week had stronger immune systems than the people who rarely went.

We should be thankful that religion has been established as a dominant approach to true beliefs.

Serpentine Tale: A True Story

As a young man, I was always interested in hiking and camping. Lake Mombasha, situated across the New Jersey border in New York, is a large lake, surrounded by majestic forests and visited by many.

On one of my trips along the Appalachian Trail, which runs through the New York area, well up in the higher portion of the mountain, I noticed there were large flat rocks on some area of the trail.

As a scoutmaster, I have spent many years in the woods and the along trails, which made me alert to my surrounding area. Now here I am, hiking along an uphill trail, and I note that one of the large flat rocks along the trail has some leaves gathered in a bunch. Ah-ha! There under the leaves is an area exposed enough to reveal a copperhead snake (not very large, probably less than four feet).

This is an example of what can happen to the unwary when going up a trail. Some inexperienced hikers have even encountered a venomous snake. Carry a long tick, sturdy enough and about six feet in length. With this pole you can flush the trail and note if there are any snakes in the bush.

But if you try to pin the snake down with either a straight stick or a forked stick, the rock under the snake will not hold the snake and it will crawl right through, so here's the trick. Cut a straight stick or use the one you use on the trail, and also a forked stick. Pin the snake down with the straight stick and when the snake rears its head, you can try using also the forked stick.

After I caught the snake, I took a string from my pocket and formed a noose, lowered it around the snake's head, and tied its body to the stick. "Jungle Jim" with this trophy, I entered the small town and was received as a hero.

Back in 1940, I had 35 boys in Troop 112. This was a tough gang. While going to the scout meetings, some of the local yokels, the wise kids, called our scouts "chippy shooters." That's all our boys needed--we roughed up a few and the episode never happened again.

People have the wrong impressions of scouts and their activities. For example, one of my friends said, "They're a bunch of sissies, running around with shorts and neckerchiefs." Well, fine, but I showed him the scout magazine which illustrated some scouts skinning a rattlesnake and cooking it. (Boy, let me have some more.)

At one of our parties a young man said that he was fearless, and that no animal could scare him. He said this just to annoy me, so I invited him on one of my trips into the top of one of our mountains. This was a weekend trip, which would give me ample time to test his mettle.

Time elapsed. There we were, just the two of us, and around the time it was beginning to get dark I left him by the campfire and went behind a large boulder to observe his brave attitude. It was not too long before the first cry of "Hey Ed, where are you?" Later, with more crescendo, he exhibited the natural fear of the unknown, yelling, "Hey Ed, don't leave me alone!" What is very interesting, as woodsmen know, is that the shadows create animal-like creatures that can make a small pine tree look like a bear.

In one of my hikes, I set my pup tent right on a deer trail and during the early hours a large deer stopped in front of my tent and snorted. I simply banged a few things in the tent, and he went away. Deer me.

About 12 boys applied for membership in Troop 4, at the Sacred Heart Church in Clifton. I lined up the boys, and as a former Signal Corps sergeant, I thought I would try a few tricks on the "greenies." I stood at attention, and yelled real loud, "Fall in!" Well, wouldn't you know, they looked at the floor, and thought I meant fall in the hole. I told them not to fear. "At the next meeting, when I yell 'jump,' don't come down until I give the orders!" Tumultuous laughter rent the air.

The Scout Patrol

In 1940, I was in charge of a group of about 28 scouts from 11 to 18 years old. This was the Scout Patrol, organized to find lost children. Each boy had to earn his own uniform. I contacted local businessmen, who hired the boys just long enough for them to earn their shirts and pants. We supplied the emblems.

I made a full size dummy of a boy, and hid it in the woods, so as to train my scouts. Whoever found the dummy was rewarded with a hunting knife or a hatchet.

Let Me Die

Don't let the government tell you what to do. Why should I wear those stupid seat belts. They muss my hair, and I feel trapped. The hard hats make me sweat. It burns me up to stop at lights or stop signs. Many times I have to wait in line behind cars when there is no one there.

Regarding smoke alarms, a friend of ours was annoyed because the smoke alarm went off in the kitchen. She took a broom, hit it real hard, and it shattered into a real mess. I told her not to worry, I would always attend her funeral.

So you go hiking, climbing, gliding, shoot the rapids, and a multitude of other things. Are you prepared for any calamity or are you an untouchable?

Its sad to see so many unprepared young people take to these sports, with no conception of the real consequences, and get into bad trouble.

Some people think that scouts are a bunch of sissies with short pants and hanging knives. They always depict the gag where a scout wants to help an old lady across the street and she becomes very angry when he tries to force her across the road. (I have been a scoutmaster for many years, but I quit that sort of thing when she hit me with her pocketbook.)

In scouting, especially the Cub Scouts, when the boys are lost the first tree they encounter they must adopt and stay put. This is their tree and no one can take it and away from them. This is a good way to keep them at one spot instead of running through the woods.

Adults as well as young people take some chances. I knew of some hunters who became lost, and wandered around in the woods with no idea where they were. They had matches, rifle, and some game that they shot, but they panicked.

Let's review a few articles that you might take along:

A lighter, or water proof matches. It is very easy to waterproof matches. Dip them in hot wax, then use a waterproof container. This is a good idea for your wallet, too. Place it in a plastic pouch.

Regarding a first aid kit, take along a pad for your heel. You will appreciate this tip, a blister can spoil your trip.

Communication: this is a very serious subject. CB Radio, telephone, whistle, marine air horn (this will give you a long range).

If I planned to spend several days to a week, I would notify the forest ranger, the local police, and even some homes in that area. I would tell them where I planned to stay, how long, and give them my home phone number. With the advent of the car phone, making sure that the batteries are fully charged and possibly carrying a spare would give me great comfort.

Making an Indian "help" fire with smoke signals takes a little training. Remember, all forests have a ranger on duty and if you make a smoke fire he will triangulate your position and help will be near.

If you feel that you are man enough, and want to protect yourself from bears or mountain lions, get a six foot pole, sharpen one end, and when you are being charged by either one, place one end under your arm and the other end against a tree, so when the animal charges he will impale himself and you can later skin him and receive some loot for it.

Make a study of snakes. Most snakes sleep during the day, and some will strike even after several people pass the snake. Carry a long stick to brush ahead of you and keep you safe.

Carry some foul weather gear. Just a large garbage bag pulled over you will keep you dry. Sit in one and we will pick you up.

Now lower the embers and let's go to bed.

Road Rage

In a class on defensive driving, the instructor asked a group of elderly women if any of them had ever noticed motorist making obscene gestures. One woman said, "Sure, I do it all the time." Aggressive drivers have become a dangerous nuisance on the roads in New Jersey, according to an article in the Herald News. Business and government representatives recently held a conference called "Watch Out." The head of the New Jersey Traffic Bureau said that aggressive driving is a factor in 28,000 fatalities per year.

He said that when people take a test on aggressive driving they always say, "Yeah, I've got to change my ways." But by the time they get into the car and get to the first intersection, they're back to blowing their horns.

Daily we read, hear, view, and note the great number of accidents and deaths. We forget that there are around 40,000 deaths each year by cars, which is not necessary. Most of these accidents could have been avoided by a little more attention to driving. Great care must be taken, especially in the small cars, which are too light and cannot withstand the impact as can the heavier cars. Let's not name the small cars "Totals" with driving rages. We must take this with a grain of salt, but remember to throw it over your shoulder.

Let's go back a few years and get ourselves a couple of horses and a wagon (or are you too young to remember the depression?).

I remember the old-time cars from when I was a small boy (sigh). They were like tanks. We felt like we were riding in the gangsters' touring cars. When I was ten, in 1925, my brother had a Graham-Paige. While on a trip in Passaic, we were hit by a small coal truck. It wrinkled our fender near the running-board (for the faint of heart, a running board was located on each side of the car and was used as a long step to enter the car), while the coal truck's front was totaled. The thickness of our car could have built two or more cars. Today, some cars appear to be going either forward or backward. Sit on the hood and so long. There won't be too many antiques from the modern car.

'Twas not the night before Christmas, but the year was 1927 and my age about 12. With a few kids of technical minds, I decided to back my brother's car out of the garage. I climbed up and settled behind the large steering wheel. I started the car and put it into gear, and slowly started backing out of the garage. All of a sudden the wind slammed the door and as I backed up I took the door right off. Lordy me! (Southern accent not mine.) After I combed down my hair, I'll show you some American ingenuity. My father had taught me how to fasten a house door when the hinges became loose. Just stick· a matchstick into the hinge hole and the screws will hold like the dickens. With the aid of my cohorts, I lifted the door in place and voilá, that was it. And the damn thing held.

Years later, in the house painting business, we were painting a house that was quite high and required a 40-foot ladder. Well, sir, we were still a few feet short, but we were not defeated. We placed the 40-foot ladder on top of the hood of the small truck, pulled the ladder up to the required point and completed the job. As they say on TV, don't try this at home, or with any new car.

My niece bought a new car and mentioned how sophisticated it was. It even informed her of the incidentals in its operation. Well, what did the car say? It said, "Don't forget the next payment."

We had our days with small cars. like the Volkswagen, sometimes called the "folks wah-gin." I have a 1961 Chevy, and I noticed that it didn't have a right side rear mirror. Why? Well, in the old days the cars were not supposed to pass on the right. Now, instead, I have a top-view mirror, in case they come over my car. Don't get a "car-de-o-graph."

Although I have not installed these items myself, during a crime watch meeting with the police I stood up and made a presentation. I suggested that no one should lock their car doors, but should leave the keys in the lock, and that no one would get away with my car. "Take heed," one woman said. "You will lose your car to carjackers." No way. As the criminal sat in the driver's seat and turned the key on, a shaft would protrude under his bottom, making for a fast exit. A police officer said that I might forget and get it myself. I responded, "Well, sir, I wear a plate."

"Fingering" was created by the Romans. Some used the finger and some used the thumb. One family went out for a ride in their shiny new car. Dad stopped at a traffic light and did not make a jackrabbit start. The "behinder" blasted his horn, and finally overtook the little family with the two kids in the back seat. As the horrible man passed them and produced "the finger," one of the little girls said, "Look, mom, that man has a boo-boo."

Road rage is nothing new, but today with the population increase we just have more screwballs on the road. Let's follow the adventures of one horn-blowing recipient. This fellow pulls up to the stop-light, and we now see that he made a mistake in stopping at the red light. Lo and behold, a died-in-the-wool blower casts his ballot, blow times four square. Our hero is not mindful at first, but when the rear-ender continues, that is enough. He steps from his car and saunters down to dopey. He lifts up the hood of the now-scared blower's car, pulls out a number of ignition wires, and with a slight bow bid this ingrate says, "Have a nice day."

Last week, I was devastated. I could hardly get over it. What did I do? I stopped at a stop light! Rage-e-ology. I do not practice road rage. In fact, they will run me off the road because I stop at stop signs, make proper U-turns, and stop at red lights and any other signals to keep me alive.

Let's put out the lights and go to bed. No horn-blowers union.

Press One

Phoney Baloney. You have reached the Ajax Battery Company. Your call is very valuable. We will record your conversation for posterity. Press one if you want to get a charge out of me. Press two if you want to speak to a negative person. Press three if you just want. After this pressing, I could do better at the cleaners.

I was on the phone in a public phone booth and noticed three young ladies waiting for me to terminate. While in this process, the operator said that I should press one, which I did. It was not the phone but one of the young ladies. Wham, bam, thank you m'am. An unpresidential response. October Red.

Outlaw cell phones. The new idea is to stop your car along the road to make a call. However, a new invention permits you to use the phone as a remote unit. Look ma, no hands. This is not too good. Some compare this to the radio and say that this could distract one's attention from safe driving. Not so: the cell call may contain exciting information, perhaps a wedding or a funeral or some romance that could cause poor driving.

While sometimes used for silly conversations, I predict that the cell phone could be of tremendous aid in reporting accidents, robberies, and many other incidents that would go unnoticed.

If there is a power failure in your home, the cell phone can get you through. But make sure that it is fully charged. Some phones can be attached to a charger that you can use in emergencies in the home.

Helpful Hints:

1. If your car breaks down on a highway or any other place and you are alone, usually someone comes to your aid, or so it seems. Use your phone even if the phone is not working. Hold it up to your ear, and now the visitor will think you are calling 911. If they are reliable, they could then call 911 for you. But don't open the car door. Don't trust them.

2. Someone might tell you by voice or gesture that one of your car tires is flat. Do not get out of the car, especially in a semi-deserted parking lot. Pull up to some other car and ask them if your tire is flat.

3. Car locked? Call the police. Shame, shame, everybody knows your name. Here is the most simple thing to do. Make a duplicate set of keys and keep it in your wallet or pocketbook. To remember where you parked in a shopping center, on your way out of the car place a paper drinking cup or handkerchief on your antenna to identify your car's position.

4. You could place a sign on the back of your car indicating there are "Booby Traps On Board."

5. A good reminder is to write down the thing you want to remember and fasten it around your car keys with a rubber band. Voilá!

Why Do We Seek the Shore?

At the beach, there are many activities enjoyed by young and old. Here we see great engineers constructing humongous and famous sand castles on every beach. Later, the relentless tide performs its destructive power of the waves. Lookey there, the kids are covering dad with mounds of sand. Wow, only his head is sticking out. We call this a "sand-a-monium." Who cares, that's our kids.

Spread around the beach is a conglomeration of research artists involved in "blanket policies," which includes sun glasses, radios blaring, buckets, games, suntan lotion, and a host of other goodies, and anything that promotes fun and relaxation.

Remember the poet who said, "And in the sky the larks still bravely singing fly"? He did not mention, Don't look up.

The science of biology. The young children soon learn the real thing in the flesh. Oops, I just stepped on a jellyfish. Regular contacts are made with the run-of-the-mill crabs, eels, starfish, and a bunch of other "stepover" creatures.

While the sun sinks into the west, everyone seems exhausted, suntanned, and not ready for love, and as we slowly leave, our gaze again turns back to the beach that we will again return to but seems difficult to leave. If thus far we have survived the sand castle, it won't be long before its demise. Look, the waves have increased in height and are rolling over the creation that we love. In one swoosh, the castles and other innovations are gone. With a few tears and sniffs of their noses, they realize that this is a temporary mode of reunification with their beloved beach. Anchors away, and again back to the salt mines, forsooth. Other groups meet new friends and promise to see them next week, weather permitting. The redundant life awaits.

A tip to the wise: Forget the Alamo, but remember the sunscreen. The unwary expose themselves to the sun on the beach, not realizing how dangerous are the rays that penetrate the skin and create burns. Another important thing to remember is that this burn may not appear until some years later. A friend of mine had skin cancer on his nose and forehead. He created this by fishing and exposure to the sun without any cover. In this case, he never wore a hat. This condition warrants numerous trips to the doctor. Make sure that the sunscreen lotion is the best. Suffer not ye little children.

Perillo Tours

Many travelers in various countries have nothing but praise for the Perillo Tours. Mr. Perillo and his staff are well-organized, and especially assist senior citizens to enjoy themselves without the usual hassle of self-appointed tours. If you desire to travel alone, you may not plan the trip to accommodate all the sights, hotels, and restaurants, and may not feel as safe as you would on a planned professional tour.

While in the Army Signal Corps and stationed in Belgium, I was fortunate that during a lull in bombing I went on some interesting trips. Our signal company moved around in five countries. We were a special group that handled all types of communications.

I visited the tomb of Napoleon, in France. This is the place of Napoleon's burial, under the done of Invalids, in Paris. The inscription above the entrance to the crypt, taken from Napoleon's will, says "I declare and desire that my ashes shall rest on the banks of the Seine, in the midst of the French people that I have loved so well." Napoleon's remains were brought there in 1840 from St. Helena (I vas dere, Charlie).

I also visited the Eiffel Tower, which is an outstanding sight to see.

While in England, people asked me if I had seen the changing of the guards. Hell no, I said. I had all I could do in changing my underwear.

Perillo has many ways to advertise. For example (my inspiration):

Perillo and son
In my heart you have won
In countries around the world
Many flags have unfurled

Perillo has yet to realize the emphasis I have placed upon his world travels and adventures, and his magnificent tours. He promised to send me abroad. As yet, no answer. I am still waiting for her.

Jamaica

It's vacation time. Do we really need escape, do we really enjoy the trip, or do we just have to be able to tell our friends what a wonderful time we had, while being on the center stage?

My wife and I decided to take a vacation on a cruise, which we had never had the opportunity to enjoy before. Our friends came to bid us bon voyage. Lots of tears and handkerchief waving. What's this gangplank? Finally on board, we enjoyed the "rigors of mortise." All is well that ends with water. If you have never taken a cruise, with its new acquaintances and heaps of food and liquor, dancing with wolves, and the lotteries galore, 'tis a far, far better thing I have done than ever before.

The ship stopped at one of the ports where we were able to get un-seabound. Go ashore and do a little shopping and much window shopping, with malaise toward none.

Women buy gifts, which I rescind, and now we have the gifts called attic storage, or laid away, gadgets. Well, anyhoo, while the wife went carousing around the glaring windows, I sat outside at one of the tables, enjoying my martini with two olives and a dash of sterilized ice cubes. While I was at rest with the rest of the world, a woman came up to my table and with some shock yelled, "Hey Ed, is that you?" I

jumped to my feet, and lo and behold, it was a former high school chum who I hadn't seen in years.
We did some "denture rattling," a few realistic
squeezes, and sat down with the old-time passages of
gone-by days.

We returned to the frivolity of the good ship
and enjoyed all the exciting productions, which created memories for years to come.

Back home, but not in Indiana, we were the
center of amazement as we enlarged on the many
satisfactions we produced. Now is the time for all
good men to fool the audience. Thusly I told them
that at times I never forget but seldom remember,
and I tried to recall the city where we met this school
chum. They tried to help me remember, but alas and
alack. I gave them a hint, I said the city's name began
with a J. Finally one said, "Jamaica?" I said, No, I
didn't make her. (Raise your hands if you get it. If
not, try again.)

The Metric System

The metric system is a system of weights and measures based on a unit called the meter. This was in our basic training as apprentices in the Forstmann Woolen Co. In our lectures, we were told that the metric system was developed by a commission of French scientific men, and was adopted in France in 1700.

All the machines in both the Garfield and the Passaic plants used the metric system in all their measurements, so that the gears, pulleys, and shafts would fit any other part of the maze of machinery.

The metric system was used on all our machinery because the machines and parts were made in Germany. As time eroded the machines we were required to purchase some American machines, and these were not metric. The problem with the new American equipment was that the gears and shafts were not universal throughout the machines. In the German machines, using the metric system, any shaft or pulley would fit anywhere throughout the plant.

So it came to pass that the kings law was the law of the land. He proclaimed that he discovered that his foot was twelve inches long. From this logarithm he devised the "Meter, meter, on the wall, who has the smallest feet of them all?" Here he put his foot in it.

Pyramids, sphinx, castles, tunnels, and under-takers all have harmony in common. With our ability to measure the planets, stars, and all the galaxies, and all space probes, I offer this axiom:

Give them an inch, they want a foot, give them a foot, they want a yard, give them a yard, they want a barbecue.

Be there a man with soul so dead that never to himself has said, You finish and depart from all.

Lincoln

Abraham Lincoln, the sixteenth president, was born in a crude cabin (but not a log cabin) in Kentucky and grew up with hardly any education. After his mother died, his father married a widow with three children, and she encouraged Lincoln in his studies, against his father's wishes. His father was later killed by Indians.

Lincoln spent less than a year in school, but he did learn to write, read, and do figures. He was a boy among boys.

He worked at home, and at other people's farms and stores. When he was 19, he went on a trip by packet boat to New Orleans. That was Lincoln's first view of slavery, and he vowed that if he ever had the opportunity he would punish the slave owners.

With nothing but the clothes on his tall back, he settled in Salem, Oregon. He studied law and gained entrance to the bar. Finally, he was offered the Oregon governorship.

We should teach our children to emulate Lincoln. Education begins in the classroom, where first impressions formulate the young minds.

Lincoln can also be remembered for his image on the penny. An article in the Herald News says that Americans have tucked away more than seven billion dollars worth of coins. One man accumulated more than a million pennies over more than fifty years of saving his change. The coins weighed more than five tons.

Some scholars say, "A penny before the eye, can obscure the light of day." I say, two cents before the eye can make you blind.

Slavery, the Curse of a Nation and of Nations

Slavery, bondage, servitude, subjugation to another or others, these are all ways to say that one person has complete ownership of another.

Franklin, Adams, Jefferson and Madison opposed slavery. Washington owned slaves but in his farewell address he expressed the hope that it might be abolished by law, and he freed his own slaves by a provision in his will.

Africa still retains remnants of the slave trade. Slavery exists in the Sudan and in Mauritania even today, according to Passaic Black activist L. Little, Jr., who says "These countries are my people." Little has a tough time ahead of him, especially since those like Louis Farrakhan deny the existence of slavery in Africa. But Little will not give up, that's not his style. Persistence is what propelled Little to the top of the Black Forum as an activist in Passaic.

Early settlers in New Jersey brought slavery to the state, and it was a slave who discovered copper in what is now Passaic County. A slave named Jack found a rock containing copper ore, and agreed to show the source to his owner, Capt. Arent Schuyler, in return for his freedom. Schuyler agreed, and later formed the Schuyler Copper Mine.

How to Select a President

The Florida voting problem has created one of the wonders of the world. Like, I wonder who's kissing her now.

The problem can be easily solved. Gore was right. He advocated that we must consider the American people, and count all the votes. Wow. Can we solve this problem?

We must count all the votes of all the fifty states. But we need help, which we can realize by the aid of Indians. That is, the American Indians, like the group of Navajos during World War II who used their language as a code. This we can use to help Gore and Bush to understand each other. These votes will be hand counted, but the quick solution is to allow each candidate to assume the office of the presidency for two years. Now they can work together to form a perfect union. It will require that time for all the ballots to be counted.

I hope that we have learned a lesson. Don't believe for a moment that this country will be devastated by any candidate. The American people are not ready to vote when the machines are not properly functioning. Perhaps we need a book entitled "How, When, Where, and Who, Or: Organized Confusion." We must realize that it is easy to be confused by the methods of voting. The average person cannot fully comprehend the complexity of modern politics.

Let's look at the story about lemmings. These are mouse-like creatures that run rampant through the countryside and number in the thousands. They eat everything edible in sight, follow their leader, and the remaining lemmings that have not been devoured by birds or other animals run over the cliffs to their death by drowning

There is some talk about making the most popular candidate the winner. What is a popular candidate? He must learn to play an instrument, do a little tap dancing, make fun out of the other fellow, and appear like a jolly comedian.

The President of the United States, the chief executive officer of the United States government, is the only official who is responsible to the whole nation. The Secretary of State and the heads of other executive departments are responsible to him and only indirectly to the people. The unique character of the president's position has made him one of the most powerful rulers in the world. Now, you can see that we need a person who has the ability to rule our United States in a serious manner and not be involved in the problems of how we elect him. All these other situations can be handled by the states and permit our president to handle major problems of state and foreign decisions.

The politicians, when quoted, say that the American people need to know. To know what? The public is still trying to find out what they are supposed to know. I believe that we have reached a pinnacle and have sat on it.

Let's sneak a peek at the candidates in action. On a quiet platform, two knights face each other. One is defending the land of his forebears, the other the honor of his crest. The other warrior screams defiance, in his right and divine providence.

Swords clash, armor rattles, the defender scores a direct hit to the other's chest, and the other knight falls to his knees. A romantic scene, plucked out of the middle ages. This is better than shouting at each other and acting like fools.

Another gesture would be to make the loser become the vice president. But what would we call them? Well, let's call them "Repo-Dems." Right or wrong, this is my country, and I have defended it by serving in the United States Army Signal Corps. God Bless America.

If I Were King

I came not to bury him nor praise him

Let's journey into the past, where kings and rulers had absolute power over life and death.

We can compare the difference between kings and presidents. A king is "a person vested with supreme powers in a foreign state, territory, or nation."

The scene is a beautiful castle, amidst rolling hills, lush pastures, and winding roads. Queen Hilary and Princess Chelsea are standing on the courtyard balcony of the grand palace. They shade their eyes against the brilliant sun. Now as they peer out over the winding road that leads to the castle courtyard they note a steady rise of dust clouds the king and his knights are creating by the thundering hooves of their steeds. Ah, Hilary points to the approaching men on horses, there is the king and his knights, so happy they survived their venture.

Our loyal king raises his hand and gestures for the drawbridge to lower, and they create an exciting entrance over the bridge as they enter the castle. The drawbridge is quickly raised as a precaution against marauding bands of criminals.

After they settle down, and their horses are rubbed down and fed, only then does he meet his family and friends to attend a great feast with the knights and their ladies. Since the king is not King Arthur, he has a rectangular table, forsooth.

Wine flows, glasses clink, and the king leans over and kisses Hilary the queen, as well as the princess. Dinner is enjoyed by all. Later they return to their chambers, except the king, who will hold court to determine the guilty or innocent and the manner of punishment.

First he proclaims that all leaks must be stopped, relegated to the proper places. He raises his scepter aloft, and the crowd assures him that he is now their king and they will obey all his requests. He now sits on the throne, and gestures for his aides to bring forth the prisoners, who consist of charlatans, quacks, and cheats who tell lies (also castle leakers and a multitude of knaves). Their punishment is very unique. The king plans the ordeal for each one of them, which could be banishment from the land, hanging, the "iron lady" torture, or a host of other goodies. He tells the knights he has just received a new shipment of torture paraphernalia from the dungeon.

Despite the king's massive power, he must vanquish all the enemies in the area of his kingdom. For example, Medusa, according to Homer one of the frightful phantoms of Hades. Hesiod mentions these gorgons Stheno, Euryale, and Medusa. All were mortal except Medusa. Their hair was entwined with serpents and their hands were of brass, their bodies covered with undentable scales. Their brazen teeth were as long as the tusks of a wild boar, and they turned to stone all those who looked upon them.

The king realizes that he must set forth this day and journey to pit his sword against the creature and capture it, dead or alive. He dons his armor, sword, and lance, and with his faithful squire at his side bids the castle inmates and his family adieu (a dew—no rain).

He crosses the drawbridge, and with flags flying and trumpets blaring he sets forth with honor and pride.

Unknown to the media, he has an instrument like a scythe, by Hermon. With various weapons like those, Perseus obtained an easy victory.

With great caution, they proceed through a vast area of desolation, forests, and heavy weeds. Suddenly the king beckons to his squire to dismount and gestures at some footprints in the sand. The squire confirms that they are made by Medusa, the terrible creature that the king must now apprehend. He tells his squire to take cover behind a large tree. The king now slowly sets forth with his horse, who had tended in many onslaughts. Hark, says the king, I just remembered that this horrible creature, the one who hit a Homer, could turn into stone anyone it sets its lid or eyes on. He whips out his cell phone and calls his optometrist and explains the turning-to-stone story. He perceives this talent because he spent one night at the Holiday Inn, where his knight supplied him with a dashing messenger who had the special formula which when worn could bisect the image of the creature's gaze like a sidewinder and cast a mean shadow, so the rat could not turn the king into stone. Medusa now had rocks in its head, and with a stone's throw the king was on the right track.

The squire, with his flute, inspired the king to get this whole mess over with, so as to cut out the flute's horrible sequences.

The monster reared its ugly head and was about to turn our king into stone. The king could now ponder his escape, if any. However, our king with his mighty sword and gadgets charged the beast and as the creature turned its head it was at just the right angle so that the king slashed the pitiful creature and whacked off its head.

The Noble Barns

Don't get excited, barns are always noble.

During the king's reign (he was always horsing around), he summoned his sew-sew constituents around him. He made them promise not to divulge the secret meetings so he would not be known by the peasants to act like this. This activity was not like "Trump's Castle," which is still a hassle. The secret barn was large enough to accommodate all this royal loyals. Perhaps it could be compared to the underground railroad. Here they could "make tracks," or the tie that binds.

Later, he sent out his pages, who finally made the book. Criers, who lamented and later were hemmed in, were promoted to "handker-chiefs." This could get worse. If there would be any confusion, can-sumption be done about it (ah-cough, ah-cough)? Taken from the art-kives.

The path was worn by walkers. Their scientists there used the arc-angels to protect the slip-artists. Security was tight. Those who entered were patted down. Even to this day, we wonder why the king won so often. Perhaps he used "spec-ter" to vanquish the non-believers.

In the days of yore, gambling was called "chancing"—like loose change. Security was at its utmost. Even in today's casinos there is a large reward for the "one-armed bandit."

If one could only see the pom-piss-ity that took place in the gambling halls of the hidden castle, the ladies with their flowing gowns, men in knitted clothes. Large amounts of money were carried by the knaves, who were formally in the knavy. (How can I stand this?)

A large sign was posted on the outskirts of the casino grounds. It read, "Post Nobles." (Still weeping.)

The king sat on a second-hand throne. From this point he wagered, posted, handed, and roused the ingrates, so they would be frightened and play ball. It's like on television, the guy who broadcasts "Hardball."

When the king was still a very young fellow, he stood outside of the castle that housed the future princess. He would yell, Con-que-bines, come out to play.

Naturally, the queen hung around with the knights, enjoying the nectar of the gourds.

All good things must come to an end—and so with the mid-evil castle, well hidden in the back woods, adjacent to the main castle. The king, in this hidden sinning place, proclaimed that all the buildings must be abandoned for lack of security. He in his heyday was known as the "Throne of Arc."

The king was later fined as a "bookmaker:
loose-leaf.

Horse Lovers, Attention

A horse is a beautiful animal., and worth the time and care allotted to its protection and health

Each fall, a horse's master set forth to obtain shelter for his prize animal. He was informed that the farmers gathered around the potbellied stove in the county store, to spin their yarns. Ah, here was the place of restitution for his horse. Here he hoped to find a farmer who was compassionate.

Summer quarters were quite adequate; however, winter was drawing cold patterns and would require immediate action. He was well aware that his horse required shelter, food, exercise and grooming. This was important.

Now is the time for all good men to start "horsing around." At first, the farmers were not interested in his horse's plight, but when they learned that his horse was a racer their attention was well focused.

Farmer #1: One of the farmers suggested a friend who would be interested. Here was ample space for the horse to run on a home-made track. On his visit to this farmer, the owner was told that his horse would be sheltered, fed, exercised, and groomed. The price was a mere one hundred dollars per month. The owner said that it was great price, but would call for the arrangements as required.

"Zilch. " Oh, by the way, the farmer was quite emphatic about keeping the manure

Farmer # 2: So back to the bargaining table. He joined the farmers in a good cup of coffee, and told them of his plight They were impressed, and one of them suggested another friend who had a large farm, and he was sure would accommodate the horse. (A friend in need, is a friend in greed.) Here was the same story: feed, exercise, grooming, shelter. The price would be seventy-five dollars per month, and again he would keep the manure (this was pure manure). The owner again burst forth with usual excuses, and went on his way.

Farmer # 3: This was the final encounter. One day he was running his horse on a local race track, when a friendly man approached him to explain his admiration while watching the horse "make track." He thanked the observer and asked him if he knew a nearby farmer who could shelter his horse. Yes, he said, by all means. He knew of a rich man whose hobby was racing, and he would send the horse owner to this farmer. Mention my name, we are great friends, he said.

The climax: The owner visited this great spread, with all the facilities that would benefit his horse. While waiting for the great decision, they reminisced about the great races, and the great jockeys.

Well sir, what decision have you made?

You told me that you would feed, exercise, groom the horse and inform your help that the horse is a special animal and needed consistent care.

Well, sir, he said, this care would cost you twenty-five dollars a month.

Hang in there, you did not tell me about keeping the manure, the owner said.

With an assured voice, the man said, for that price, there won't be any manure.

Lemmings

Lemmings can tell you the truth. We as humans have reached a pinnacle, and have probably sat on it.

I think that the mattress company, "Have more fun in bed," has the right idea for overpopulation. We are running out of space, running out of water, running out of patience. We watch the multitude grow and grow, until we don't know where to settle them.

I am not an untouchable, but I imagine myself sitting in a void, surrounded by flying obstacles of religions, crowds, cults, and a myriad of beliefs. Each is trying to prove that it is the best.

The human race is still in a period of evaluation. We are still up in the trees, we are still in the tower of Babel. We cannot communicate with each other. Our stupid manner of handling the presidential affair is very childish. I believe that we should go back to the olden days when men had several wives. The thought makes me shudder with glee. Wow.

So, where do we go from here? Just sit on your rump and let George do it.

We doodle with color. Oh, he is blue, he is green, he is sky-blue-pink, so what? I wish those people who despise another's color would wake up some day and assume another. Just imagine, it even now makes you shudder.

In writing this thesis I realize that I am so smart it frightens me to no end.

Now, the bombshell:

We scan the news and are aghast to read that many people were killed in plane crashes, bombings, volcanoes, and all sorts of events. But do you know what a car is? No? Well, it is very easy to commit "Harry Carry," forty thousand or more people killed yearly.

Laugh and Live Longer

Dr. Steve Allen, Jr., son of the comedian and a professor of family medicine, said that for patients with high blood pressure he prescribes laughter. "My prescription is that you should laugh and act silly at least twice a day."

We will confirm that Dr. Allen's advice is very important, and by recognizing the signs we can help each other. A friend of mine, while riding with others in a car, noticed that the driver was high strung and very nervous while driving, and advised him to cool down before some accident could happen. The driver was also told at the hospital to do the same, while being treated for some stomach problems. While driving, he would come to a red light and yell at it to turn green. Alas and alack, on another occasion, while driving by himself, he had a heart attack and died at the scene.

I asked some friends of mine if they had every heard of Johnny Appleseed. Naturally, most everyone has heard of him. Well, I told them that I, too, played a part in the fantasy. Now they call me "Eddie Make-em-laugh." I do make it a practice to leave people in a state of humor.

Frustration seems to be everywhere. My sister's lady friend was in the kitchen when all of a sudden the smoke alarm went off. She balanced the kitchen broom and with one perfect shot slammed it to the floor, where it fell into a thousand pieces. I then asked her who her funeral director was, so I could not be late for the next episode.

While most people know about "road rage," there seem to be many more types of rages. For example, the supermarket has lots of adventure, with flying shopping baskets sailing into some cars, while the perpetrator ignores his cart's flying mission of banging into another car. So what?

While shopping in one of the markets, we were lined up about six deep and the man in front of me was losing his cool. But I calmed him down by saying that he did not need this stupid system of waiting. He asked, "What do you suggest?" Well, let's get out of this line and go home and buckle up with our hunting gear and go out into the great beyond called the woods and shoot a few animals and take them home and on the way stop at the fruit stand and purchase some items and go home, and wait until your wife skins them and makes a wonderful meal. So you see, we don't need this standing in line and wasting our time. He was aghast, and now became like a little kitten. He fully realized that we are all very fortunate that we have a system that places all these items right at our disposal.

Post office nonsense: So there he stood, raving about the two cent increase in the postage stamps. Here was another poor suffering person who needed aid, and so I agreed with him and said that he did not need to be insulted by these increases. He said, "All they are delivering is a simple envelope." What can we do? I solved the problem. I said, let me take your letter to California and it will be simple. All you have to do is pay for the gas, motel, and my time, and there you are. He finally revived, and forever held his peace, like Forever Amber.

Read my story about Sonny Bono, who kept the Congress in humor. His contribution was to keep them laughing so that they didn't have time to pick on each other.

I heard the cry in the wilderness, and it said, "For crying out loud."

Sonny Bono: Goodbye to a Friend

Actor and congressman Fred Grandy said, "One thing you can say about Sonny Bono, he succeeded in two of the hardest industries in this country, show business and politics."

Sonny had this great sense of awe and wonderment. (This awed to be good.) I believe that if Sonny had survived, he would have said, "I was barking up the wrong tree."

Some people go around with such faces, my mother would say that if their face froze Barnum and Bailey would hire them. I could never have made it without her.

One day I told a friend a series of jokes. After a great performance, I was ready for the onslaught. I watched for some facial expression, but to no avail. Perhaps his brain did not coincide with his fibrovascular bundles, whatever those are. Oh: there is now a methodically confirmed neuron pulse. Ah: here we go, the great stone face is about to embark on his first hilarious laughter. It seems that the lower lip is slightly curled while the upper lip veers off to the right. I'll buy that, even if it is like bleeding a rock. In his eyes I did notice a little twinkle. I could never confirm that here I have created any meaning, like "uproarious laughter rent the air." What price glory. With a chuckle, I finally departed.

Great men like Sonny Bono have given us great sayings, namely "I got you babe."

Here are a few more:

Don't shoot until you see the whites of their eyes

Don't give up the ship

The Marines have landed

We have just begun to fight

Wait till the sun shines, Nelly, but when the sun goes down, bring out the moonshine

Who hit Nelly in the belly with a flounder?

What did General Custer say when he sat up straight in his saddle and put his hands on his forehead to shade it from the sun"? He said, where did all these @#&!$ Indians come from?

And last but not least, If at first you don't suck-seed, try chewing it.

Reader's Digest said that when Sonny Bono was mayor, he earned $1,500. Later, he made $2,200.

We decided to follow Bono on his goodwill tour. This happened in Jolly Olde England. We now wait outside the beautiful church. Ah, here he comes, with his coat on his arm, for it is a very warm summer day. He enters the church, sits in his pew, and prepares for a heartrending sermon. His attention is fixed on a man whose job is to keep all good people awake during the sermon. Unbelievably, this man has a long pole which has some feathers attached. When he notices someone asleep he reaches over and tickles their nose. Bono has never seen this type of a "grand awakening from slumber."

In the colonies, there were practices that were brought over from England, as we saw in the old churches. Bono did not like this old type of rude action by the church. He remembered the story of Lincoln, when he traveled up the river and saw the slave trade. (Lincoln was very angry, and said, "If I ever have the opportunity to stop this shameful trade, I will hit them hard.")

Back to the feathered sonnet (a poem that has 14 lines, so what?).

Sonny, now a senator, thought it would be a good idea to review the featheration, to get a point of view. Sonny always had good connections with the leaders, and after he told them they agreed to back him up. The issue was presented to Lord Plushbottom, who told the Bishop, and by the merits of the vote of confidence the plan was approved as presented. The king was thrilled to learn of this jolly Bono-factor. Yes, a man with a plan. The King wasted no time to bring about a proclamation:

> *Here ye, here ye*
> *Feather not your bed*
> *But only your "4-feathers"*

Nursery Rhymes

Sonny Bono and I, being of sound mind, have portrayed nursery rhymes as inherent folklore that requires a compete and new reservation. Yes, we both agreed that these rhymes were antiquated and should carry a more humorous version. All systems go.

Fee, Fi, Fo, Fum, I smell the blood of an English-man. Be he alive or be he dead, I will grind his bones to make my bread.

As a kid, I was devastated by this bloodless venture. When I told some people that for a long time I did not eat bread, they felt sorry for me. I was born and bread, and loaded it with jelly.

Metamorphosis. *Little Miss Muffet, sat on her tuffet, eating her curds and wheys. Along came a spider, and sat down beside her, and frightened Miss Muffet away.*

Now that we got rid of the spider, I called Miss Muffet on the web. I said, Now, now. Dot, calm. But young lady is there nothing else for you to do but tuffeting? Who ever heard of curds and wheys. Go fetch a broom and do some flying, or something. Already, she was quite perturbed, and said, "I'll huffet and I'll puffet, and blow the man down." But later she became a saleslady and sold some "Tuffet-ware."

Jack be nimble, Jack be quick, Jack jumped over the candlestick.

It shows to go you. What happened? He jumped over the candlestick, and pow! His foot got caught on the stick, and the candle produced a flaming mess, which soon burned the house down. On a thorough investigation, we noted that there were no smoke alarms or fire extinguishers, no fire department, nor any escape routes.

I hate to say this, but thousands of homes are burned down because of tallow-minded kids.

Mary, Mary, quite contrary, how does your garden grow? With silver bells and garden shells and parents with lots of dough. (Or with silver bells and cockle shells and adjoining neighbors in a row.)

Little Bo Peep has lost her sheep, and can't tell where to find them. Leave them alone and they'll come home, wagging their tails behind them. Is this a shepherd without a cane? Don't know where to find them, but do they come home? If I told them once, I told them a thousand times, she should have had a cane, trained dogs, proper supervision, the whole lot. Also, there were many wolves around to make passes. For naught. A few sheep wandered off and the kidnappers stole them and had them cloned.

Johnny Appleseed was instrumental in spreading apple seeds throughout the nation. It's well known that people planted apple seeds, grew orchards, and ate the apples, but not many people

know they also made liquor from it, so there was in-
centive to raise apples. (Into the alley and over the
fence, I got the pail, who's got ten cents. I remember
the days when you could very easily buy beer for that
amount.) They call me Eddie Make-em-laugh.

Updated: *Old Mother Hubbard went to the cupboard, to get her dog a Bono. When she got there the cupboard was bare, and Cher said that was a no-no.*

*Sonny Bono, lemon pie, kissed our Cher and made her
cry. When the senators came out to play, it was Sonny Bono's
"play of the day."*

I wish the family the best, and I always watch
any news or events that portray these fine people.
God bless.

Scatterbrain

Note: When someone tells you that they are sorry, ask them if they changed their name.

Hearing is believing: I asked a friend if she heard President Roosevelt last night on radio. No, she said, what did he say? "Ah hate wah, Eleanor hates wah, an ah hate Eleanor." She said, "I am afraid I did not hear him." And the ram parts we watch. This really is gullibility personified.

X--Rated: A proud father whose business had improved decided to send his wife and daughter to Florida. Next item on the agenda was packing. Naturally, they were both pleased about going, so they began the task of packing. Finally the time arrived for them to go. With great fanfare they "God Blessed" and hugged, and were off to the great adventure.

Home alone, dad was in charge of all the house affairs, such as the unmanly chores of household duties. Why do we men have to suffer thusly? After a good day's work of housekeeping, he finally went to bed.

A few days later, the bell rang and he answered it, only to find two familiar subjects in the role of his wife and daughter. Both appeared sullen and pale. Being an understanding man, he ap-

proached the problem with poise. He could not believe that two grown women could goof up in this
manner.

Now comes the question: What happened?
First we hear from the mother, who said, "We tried
to avoid any contacts but we got the clips." The
daughter immediately corrected the mother. "Oh
mother, it was the claps." So mother said, "What's
the difference, we both got it."

Rub-a-dub-dub, who needs to be scrubbed?

Letter from a hillbilly mother (author unknown)

Dear Son,

I'm writing this real slow cause I know you can't read very fast.

We don't live where we did when you left. Your daddy read in the paper that most accidents happen within twenty miles of our house, so we moved.

I won't be able to send you the address because the family that lived here before us took the house numbers with them so they wouldn't have to change their address.

This place has a washing machine. The first day I put four shirts in, pulled the chain, and I ain't seen them since.

It only rained twice last week, three days the first time and four days the second.

You know that coat you wanted me to send you? Aunt Sue said it would be too heavy to mail with them big buttons on it, so we cut them off and put them in the pockets.

We got a letter from the funeral home. They said if we don't make the last payment on grandma's funeral bill, up she comes.

Your sister had a baby this morning. I ain't heard whether it's a boy or a girl, so I don't know if you're an uncle or an aunt.

Your uncle john fell in the whiskey vat. Some men tried to pull him out, but he fought them off, so he drowned. We cremated him and he burned for days.

Three of your friends went off the bridge in a pick-up. One was driving, the other two were in the back. The driver got out. He just rolled down the window and swam to safety. The other two drowned. They couldn't get the tailgate open.

There's not much news this time, nothin much happened.

Love,

Mama

A Parrot's Dilemma

A young couple in an apartment decided to take a vacation. Since they could not take their parrot, they asked the super to look in on the parrot and also give the key to the plumber who said he would repair the kitchen sink. This was no problem.

Quickly packing, they took off for their trip. Incidentally, they never took the time to train the parrot, but it knew a few words, like "Hello" and "Come in."

When the plumber arrived at the apartment, he knocked on the door. The parrot answered, "Hello." The plumber yelled, "It's the plumber," but no one opened the door. He knocked again, the voice said "Hello," and he shouted "It's the plumber," but still no one came.

The plumber finally knocked on the super's door and the super gave him the key. When the plumber opened the door to the apartment, the parrot, in a loud and clear voice, said, "Hello, come in." The plumber was so surprised to hear the voice that he ran over to the sink. In so doing, he tripped on the old rug and hit his head on the floor, and there he rested. It was a coincidence that the couple came home at the right time.   The wife ran over to the plumber and yelled "Who is this?"

The parrot, also in a loud and clear voice, yelled "It's the plumber."

Thor, God of Thunder

The ancient Scandinavians represented the "God of Thunder" as wielding a mighty hammer.

So it came to pass, on a beautiful sunny day, that a giant cloud was passing overhead. There on cloud nine was our hero, Thor himself. He peered over the edge of the cloud, and boy, what did he see? Yes, it was a beautiful country girl. It is my duty to interview her, he thought, from whence cometh my health.

Landing his cloud, he tied it up to a hydrant next to the barn. He slid off and wandered over to her. Well, little girl, pray what is your name? She smiled and informed him that she was called Daisy May. (I hope so.)

He asked her if she had any trouble in finding the needle in her haystack. Yes, she said, it was in vein. Have no fear, Dr. Thor is here. Since they both saw eye to eye, he adjusted his mighty hammer and they both entered the barn. Needless to say, no success that time. Perhaps we will try again, he said, leering.

Thor became quite restless. He had the urge to merge and set his compass due north and headed for the loft. He again peered over the cloud and had a fixation on the barn (I think he was getting hammer-oids). This is awful, but on the subject we can now proceed.

This time he told Daisy that the needle in the haystack would implement the reworking of his compass. Needless to say, they both again entered the barn. This time it was eye to eye, a learned pupil. Back on his serious cloud he again coasted around the farms. He did not know exactly what he would ask her to do, but he would try.

Dear readers, 'tis not for the faint of heart, so if you falter, stop here and continue to read my book and weep no more.

We will now close with the famous saying that transpired: He is now confronting Daisy and says, "I'm Thor, remember me?" She says, "YOU'RE thor? I can't even pith." For shame.

Penny Crone's Adventures

Each night, our family takes the fifth. That is, we watch Penny Crone on Channel 5. One night some screwball made comments not fitting for a TV show. I murmured, Why don't you crawl back under your rock. Ah-ha! This was my cue to write about the rock.

Not since the "big bang" have we listened to such news referring to constant bombarding and to being invaded by flying meteorites and other fragments from outer space. Most of these objects burn up in our atmosphere and become harmless because of the protective zone between the ground and outer space. Way back many years ago it was like Orson Welles's War of the Worlds, but it was a true event. Scientists said that a large asteroid was heading towards the earth, and they did not know if it would hit us. Like the Orson Welles story on the radio, people were in a panic.

An article in the Herald News mentioned that a near miss could occur in thirty years. A mile-wide asteroid was the most dangerous one found so far. It has enormous destructive potential. Steve Moral, of the American Astronomical Society, said it would take "several years of observation" before experts are sure of its path. This is really the first "big one" to pass to close to earth.

The story of the rock: This event took place several years ago. A sizeable rock-like object, much larger than any rock in the near vicinity, penetrated our atmosphere in the area of a farmer's land. He was plowing his field when all of a sudden there stood this unearthly boulder. Hey, what the heck is that. He went over to this giant object, took out his knife, and tried to scrape off some part of the bolder to determine its contents. Begorry and begeeze, what on earth? Or should I say, Heavens forbid. Not a scratch resulted from his scraping. It's time to get some help, 'tis beyond my comprehension, by golly.

He reported it to the local gendarmes, who also tried to make tests of its composition, but to no avail. They then notified the Smithsonian Institution. These professional men had the scientific equipment to determine its composition. They extracted a small portion of the rock and shipped it back to the laboratory.

Rock of Ages, the news spread like wild fire. Scientists from all over the world became involved. Rock hounds littered the area. Some men came from Egypt (it peer-a-mid that way). Rock tests were taken as well as stress tests, one if by land and two if by sea.

The United States, as well as all other countries, awaited the outcome. There were songs and magic made to enhance the project. TV played it up. Finally the greater minds achieved a culmination of painstaking calculations and reached a conclusion that the rock contained Penny-Crone-Meum. When I told this story to a friend of mine, she hoped that they could remove the rock so that the farmer could plow again. (From a rock-a-teer, Ed Kurtz.)

The Lion's Barbiturate

Wouldst thou view the lion's den
Search afar from haunts of men
Where the reed-encircled rill
Oozes from the rocky hill
By its verdure far described
Mid the desert far and wide
    --Thomas Pringle

The lion, one of the strongest and most ferocious wild animals, is known as the "lord of the jungle." The largest lions are three feet high and more than nine feet long, weighing 500 pounds. Lions hunt their prey chiefly at night, but sometimes hunger will send them out hunting in the daytime. Don't take your glasses off, because the following is a real humdinger. (At times, I feel so smart that it frightens me.)

The story begins in a remote area of Africa, where the lion is master of the plains. Two lions who had become great friends over many a kill decided to escape the dull routine of fighting for a living and decided, Let's go into the human habitat and get a few beers. They knew of a place that was just to their liking, so off they went.

It was a little tavern by the side of the road, so they both pulled up to the bar and made themselves comfortable. I was quite fortunate that I had left the bar a few minutes earlier. I would have been a victim if I did linger.

One of the lions was still very hungry, so he up and jumped over the bar and ate the barmaid. The lion became quite ill, and ordered a barbiturate with his drink. He sat at the bar and his face became white with indigestion. In a very weak voice, the ill-fated lion meekly asked his companion what went wrong.

His friend answered, "It was the bar-bitch-you-ate."

Sex

Fancy meting you here. Don't go away. This subject will revolutionize, like the wheel industry. Without sex, there would be—nobody. Lean close, I don't want anyone to hear this. Readers, caution, be advised. As a young man, and I assure you that this same question arose among all the young, I wondered why people went to bed together. From what I heard, they perform what I learned is called sex. How could they? As Roosevelt said, A dastardly thing. I am also told that this union performed by parents results in conceiving children. Hey, hold it. What happened to the wayward stork? That was much simpler than this so-called wrestling match. How could they? Can we say, Is this the urge to merge?

Kissing is quite unnecessary, it will culminate in wild gestures and create a horizontal concept. If you practice the "soul kiss," be careful of the dentures. Haven't you heard of the jaw breaker? Also be careful of the entrance to Florida—there is a place called "Kiss-uh-me," but don't do it, it's the place of evil.

Hand shakes. In our sexual life, contact is more important than communication, so you extend your hand in a goodwill gesture and shake hands with the recipient, who tickles your palm. You pause and say, What now? Do you withdraw, does your heart beat faster? Be careful, it's like palm reading, and it will put the finger on you. This maneuver reminds me of the unemployment office. When one collects compensation while out of work, they ask you are you willing and able to work?

The wink can have a sinister eye-ball meaning—it could mean that you desire an implant.

Today's mattresses, so well advertised, will not condone the fact that you can sleep on any mattress. In the old days, the mattress was used to hide some money or treasured articles. Since the only method of heating our home was large coal stove in the kitchen, this induced early retiring in the bed with the goose-filled pillows and bed covers. Explanation is not necessary.

A sex gauge? It goes to show you how far society has advanced. Who would have imagined that sex could be measured by some sort of dang-fangled unit. Well, Jocko, in my research I see that this invention can measure the latitude and longitude. After many bed-ridden investigations, I found that it was called a sextant. Wow. Although this unit is a "measuring device used in the measuring the angular distance, especially the altitudes of the moon or stars at sea, in determining latitude or longitude," this was altered slightly to be used by the stiffening of the solar complex.

In the colonial days, it came to pass that the term "sparking" came into being. A girl would place a candle in the window to signify the welcome (father approval) of the boyfriend. The couple was then permitted to occupy the same bed, because of the cold nights. The fire was banked to preserve fuel, then father placed a board between them. I do believe that some of today's athletes would not have put up with this nonsense, and overcome the obstacle. This was an agony for both of the recipients. It was also known as the "thousand and one nights." While reading the stories of the colonial days, I began thinking about this silly "in-between board." Well, sir, if I had been the sparker, I would have brought along a knotty pine board. Either way, I would not have been "board." I do believe that if the old man had invented this new-fangled board, he would have used it.

There are wonderful stories relating to the old colonial days. For example, Captain Miles Standish said to John Alden, I will take you on a foursome. Alden asked him, What is a foursome? Well, Miles said, if they don't, we force 'em.

It was interesting to note an article in the men's magazine "Men's Health" that said a healthy sex life can make relationships more durable and better able to weather the glitches of married life. It also says that sex can be the "road to wellness." Some critics might claim that a woman's watchfulness comes from some perverse need to act like the man's mother. I deplore such skepticism. Rather, on behalf of the men of America, I suggest you file a request for more health benefits from the woman in your life. Now, if you can just figure out how to get your HMO to pay for it.

A great exposure, now all I have to do is keep a stiff upper lip.

Great World Predictions

We often hear of the predictions of the great Nostradamus. Now in the year 2000, we will hear from the Great Kurtz-a-Dumb-Mus. Ouch. So it came to pass, yes, but it's too fast. Let's gaze into my crystal ball, and bat out a few.

> *Mirror, mirror on the wall*
> *Who is the ferrous of us all?*
> *Oxide, oxide, rah-rah-rah*

My predictions are based on physiological metatarsi. If you find out what this means, let me know.

1. The world will continue to revolve at approximately 1,000 miles an hour. This movement can replicate all scientific predictions and confirm that the world is not flat. Although it may not be my belief, I still don't go too far from home. Here is an easy way to confirm this theory: just jump up in the air but make certain that you clear the highest mountain. Stay up there until the spinning world returns to the exact spot whence it came. Now come down and the case is clear. The world, though lopsided, is fairly round.

2. I will win the lottery, or as they call it, the Power Ball. But doubts begin to proliferate in this, my brilliant mind.

3. Some day athletes will either be knighted or given the title of saint. Imagine, calling Hey, Holy Joe. The only fan that I am interested in is the electric fan. Uh-basa-ball. I believe that sports is like a cult, as in, He cult have made it to third base.

Don't go away, there's more to follow. Or as they said in the old days, Don't touch that dial.

Many dentists who were not considerate of their patients were called "ruthless."

4. Scientists predict that we will experience some catastrophic changes in the atmosphere. They feel that the earth is warming by significant degrees each year, and will create massive flooding throughout the universe. There are numerous opinions of this cause of the heating of climatic conditions, but as yet no one is quiet certain of its cause and natural changes. Perhaps we can follow some changes and manifestations and begin to rally to the cause, if there is any hope left to pursue. Let's forge ahead.

I Was Awarded Sir Knight

During the Second World War, I served my basic training at Camp Crowder, Mo. This was a Signal Corps training camp. After basic, I became an instructor in radio theory and code. My other duties were instructing the art of booby traps and bayonet practice, as well as handling a rifle.

We traveled on our liberty ships, about 240 in number, and after eleven days we arrived in Jolly Olde England. In England, the brass did not have specific orders for us, so we stayed at a camp. We were quartered in tents, with mud around us, while several hundred German prisoners were quartered in nice warm buildings. The reason was that we were to move out at any time. During the day, we had to march the prisoners to a train station where they would load or unload the material for the troops. Each one of us had to take about forty prisoners and march them to their assigned jobs. The lieutenant called my name to take a group. Since my name is Kurtz—although I am Hungarian—the prisoners really perked up.

At this camp, an organization of specialists was formed. It consisted of types of men well versed in their line, that is, linesmen, telephone operators and repairers, radio and code men, cooks, and all the necessary material for the self-contained group. We were self-sufficient, having trucks, armament, various caliber larger weapons. In fact, when we arrived in England we had all this equipment to travel with and operate as required.

From this camp we finally received orders to move out. For the last time, we searched each prisoner for any weapons that could inflict damage to us or our equipment. (These men had no intention of escaping. We treated them like guests at the Waldorf. One of the prisoners asked me about Dick Tracy. You see, he had been to America several times. War is hell.)

It was during one of these field trips that my captain assigned me and four other men to take a perilous journey into the German enemy lines to perceive any new movement by their troops. I wondered why I was selected, perhaps I would learn of this event later. The men who went with me knew the German language fluently. We received all sorts of maps and guided information to enable us to travel safely. We had special equipment such as listening devices and recorders, and also our armament.

Half walking and half crawling, we went deep into the enemy territory, moving carefully so as not to be detected. After several hours, we heard some voices coming over our sensitive equipment. The men alerted me that the voices were from the German high command. We froze and set up all our listening devices and recorded the entire plan for the next onslaught. This was a hair raising situation, quiet as a mouse.

We packed up and returned to our lines, safe and sound. We were very proud of ourselves for gathering this important tactical information needed by our officers.

I was summoned to headquarters to complete the special orders as now required by British intelligence.

Here I was at the British High Command in Jolly Olde England. I was led into an office where the meeting was to take place. One of the officers asked me to make myself comfortable, so I sat in a large plush chair. On the wall I noticed very large maps of the territory I had covered in my mission.

The plot thickens. When the high officials entered the room, the first thing I had to promise them was to remain silent and not repeat any incident I was engaged in, perhaps until after the war was over. More sweat. The officer said he was also proud that I could enter the enemy territory and gather all the vital information that was so important to our allies. After a brief period I was whisked away in a large limousine.

We arrived at the king's castle only to find them waiting in the waiting room to outfit me in the proper garb necessary for a future knight.

I was told to prepare for the meeting of the King of England. The king beckoned me to approach the throne. He directed me to kneel. With sword in hand he directed the point of the sword upon my shoulder and pronounced me Sir Edward the Turd or was it fourth or should I take the fifth?

The next day the populace was informed of my great deeds of valor. They did not know the entire story until later. After learning of my activities, the royal subjects began a great parade, colorful floats, dancing in the streets. The heralds heralded, the criers cried, and all hail broke loose.

After the war I arrived home, and no one could believe the events that took place in England. I placed my new sword on the fireplace, but was very careful to keep the pointed end down so as not to come in contact with Santa Claus.

The Eyes Have It

During my basic training at Camp Crowder, Mo., a routine physical turned up a small growth in my left eye. My next appointment was at the army base hospital. The operating major, an interesting fellow, wanted to put me at ease. Well, soldier, what has caused this plight? With malice towards none, I was very pleased to see that the Army permitted me to express myself. "Well, sir, this one evening as I attended a movie, I had my eye on a fellow's seat, and he sat on it."

After my overseas duty, the war being over, I returned to the good old USA. The next problem was to obtain an implant in my left eye, the same old eye. Incidentally, the right eye also had an implant, but to this day has given no trouble. Back again to the left eye, for some undetermined reason it gave me a serious problem. I seemed to have lost my sight, for I could only view about less than half an inch. My doctor rushed me to a specialist who had to tie up the nerve endings. I spent nine days there in the hospital. Back at the ranch, this left eye now had a vision of about 60%.

With a drum roll, we move into the realm of eye-dol-ogy, forsooth.

As a house painter, one day I was sweeping off a garage roof when all of a sudden the broom came up out of nowhere and hit me square in the eye. Yes, my endangered species, suddenly it was the same old eye as it used to be!

Naturally, I closed up shop and sauntered over to the eye man. What gives? I queried. He stroked his beard, tottered a little, and said, "Man, when the broom hit you in the eye, it moved away from the pan area, readjusted its position, and a better focus predominated." At this moment, I was under the impression that I would be highlighted in the science magazine and become a celebrity.

I was beside myself (what the hell does that mean?). Before the incident, my left eye had a sight of about 70%. but now the vision improved to about 90%. Also, before, if I touched the eye it was painful, but not anymore. Another plus for me was that when I viewed a face it no longer seemed a little blurred. It was very distinct.

After the exam, I suggested that the doctor set up a sign reading, Broom Aid.

The eye is a terrible thing to destroy. Some wise men say, A penny before the eye can blot out the light of day. I say, Two pennies before each eye can make you blind.

Kevorkian

I won't trouble you with the stories that now circulate about Dr. Kevorkian assisting people to die with some dignity and stop the terrible suffering that they have to endure, the pain that never seems to end. Only those who have the problem know its enduring pain.

Kevorkian's terminally ill patients and their relatives know only too well that he was thanked for ending this horrible situation.

How do we get into these situations? Well, I don't think that it is only one particular cause that we can pinpoint. Rather, it is the way we live. I recall, when a young boy, people died from simple problems that they could not identify. If someone had a stomach ache, well, it was simply gas. We did not have all these pills or specialists, just a doctor who made house calls only when he was summoned. Naturally, we did not have any serious illness, no way. Hence the funerals.

When I tell people this story, it really seems unbelievable. But here goes:

I lost almost everything. What's the use? How can I continue the exist with all these problems? Night and day, you are the one for me (from the song). Friends, what are friends for, when not even one shows up.

I still had my old clunker of a car, and now it came in handy.

I entered the garage, closed the doors, sat in the car, turned on the radio, started the car, and what do you know. I ran out of gas.

Speaking about gas, during the gas shortage I pulled up to the pumps and told the attendant to fill it up, or else. You should have seen the contracted muscles of his face begin a convulsive upheaval. With a loud voice, he yelled real effortless, Or else what? Well, I said in a loud voice just above a whisper, Or else give me five gallons. Don't ever be timid, stand up for your rights, even if they carry you away. The sad part is that this can cause car-de-ac arrest.

The Demise of Ant-Tracks

Come out, come out, wherever you are. Stand up for your rights, even if it's your last. Perhaps I can shed some light on this fearful agent, namely ant-tracks, which has left us with a jelly fish complex.

I try to keep my house in order, water and cut the lawn, and take care of exterior problems as soon as possible. During this carousel, I came to a screeching halt, and there along the house's foundation were the famed ant tracks. I followed these tracks along the base and again stopped short to view a powderlike substance that was the residue of termites. Termites do not leave tracks, as do ants. Please note that termites leave a tremendous amount of damage throughout the nation, they eat away any wooden foundation and cannot be noticed until the damage is prominent. Now is the time for all good men and ladies to call in the gendarmes, better known as the insect demeanors. They will explain the actions of these insects and teach one how to recognize their movements to forestall future damage.

Termites do not live in houses, but eat the goodies in the wood and take it back to their lair (den).

We have millions of "track-o-neons" who have reported sightings of the powder from these ants.

For you hardy souls who believe in reincarnation, lend an ear, for we have a little carnage for you to ingest. We have contacted the "spirit-tus-u-neom" who can recall the dead who have begone from whence and their cup runneth over. These gifted wand and illusionists can bestow the very wish of the beholder. To the believer, these are not ghost-like creatures, but take on lifelike images.

At one of the séances, we asked the ghostologist to produce Sherlock Holmes and Dr. Watson. We knew that these two, who have solved many of the great, important crimes, could help us with this devastating curse.

The mystics finally produced the great Holmes and Dr. Watson, and as we sat around the table we explained the entire situation. Holmes was very attentive to the whole story, stroked his chin, and said, By Jove, Watson, let's take a powder, which they did, after a cup of tea, the tradition of the English.

We again met at an undisclosed meeting place, to keep this "under the hat," and Holmes finally, with his enlarging glasses, produced the real reason we have ant tracks.

I related the story at my home and the tracks and the powder escapade, which Holmes analyzed.

He found that the ants and the termite powder formed a chemical reaction to produce the so-called ant tracks. I asked him how he had reached such a quick conclusion, and he said that he spent one night at the Holiday Inn.

I congratulate the media for its intense endeavor to assist in solving the plight of those infected with this curse. Let's remember that we must not take things for granted, as they do in asking who is buried in Grant's tomb.

Three of the most devastating problems we have in this country are drinking, tobacco, and automobiles, among many others. We are very brave when we practice any or all of these tragedies. For example, just with our cars alone we have 40,000 deaths and many more injuries each year.

We can do something, but are very lax in solving these problems, and just go on with our daily chores. What can we do to cut down this unnecessary tragedy? First, bomb all the tobacco fields, drink up the alcohol, smash all the cars (not mine) and turn the metal into more progressive materials. Remember the road-ragers. This is a breed that when you meet them anywhere they are most pleasant people. But when called upon to commit mayhem, they are ever ready with the finger salute.

What will happen to all of us if we eliminate all these goodies? Well, without alcohol, we will not sterilize wounds, without tobacco we will disrupt the tax system. Without cars, we will learn what our families went through in the good old days. My family remembers when we took a bus from Garfield to Passaic. Trolleys were here, but did not travel too far. There were horse-drawn buggies (light carriages), few cars. We walked to work and schools, had kerosene stoves and lights, coal stove in the kitchen, and the good old outhouse, sometimes a two-seater. No heat at night, except the large feather bed covers. Morning came, and who was to get up and start the fire in the great stove? Washing was done by a "scrub-a-dub" method, heat the water since we had no electricity, no gas, pour the water, hot, into a tub and scrub away. Doctors were rare, but some made house calls, as did Santa. The ice box, now known as the refrigerator, kept a large block of ice, which contained a pan on the bottom to catch the dripping ice water.

All is not lost, for we can bring back the horse and wagon. So how, pray tell? Oh no. Yes, yes. It's easy, just hitch up the horse to the wagon, take a trip, return home, unhitch him, rub him down, feed him, make sure the straw is fresh in the barn.

Strung out. Eons have passed since the phenomenal conception of our origin, from the episode of Adam and Eve. We note that the transformation of the rib to ever has resulted in the ribbing of not only Eve but the ribbing of our women. Some call it the shaft. This intellectual metaphor is like, "I met-a-four of the kindest people around town."

Daily proponents. Consider:
I'm Sorry
Well, did you change your name?

Take care, it's only me

I lost my carriage
There are always miss-carriages here each week.

The son at college, fun and games, girls galore. Parties, romances, the lot. He decided to inform his father that the day had arrived and it's time to send him a letter. We must remember he was taking some time out from these duties around school. Here goes:
Dear Dad, No mon, no fun.
Dear Son, Too bad, so sad, your Dad

Yours truant, Ed Kurtz.

Florida, Right or Wrong, My State

The voting in Florida created some chaos, not because they did not understand the technique but because they used the wrong voting paper.

In the early days of the rise and fall of Florida, and after the insurgents were subdued, the loyalists formed a group of citizens who deemed it necessary to search the area for items that might have been left by the invaders. Some of the things they found could be used by the people, but there was one item found that was of great interest. It was a large package unusual in this area. They removed this package and placed it on a table in one of the buildings for examination. On its opening, they found a large amount of paperlike material. None of the natives knew of its nature, so they brought in a few learned men to analyze the queer looking paper. On examination, they found it to be some foreign material. In fact, they learned that it was a material known as papyrus. This was the material then used for their records. The paper was prepared from the pith of a plant. It was laid together, soaked, and dried. They now know that this plant, when prepared, was used by ancient Egyptians, Greeks and Romans for manuscripts.

There was great joy. However, care must be taken to guard against any vandalism. This papyrus material was then manufactured into the proper use for the voting system.

Night followed day, or whatever comes first, and the grand voting was instituted into a system called "voting." The irregularities were undetected until the new candidate was in office, then all hell broke loose. Pandemonium broke the sound barrier. Can you imagine, the papyrus or paper was used in modern times to elect a president.

All this hullabaloo would have been avoided if they had set up pictures of each candidate, on opposite walls, and voters would have made no mistake in identifying their choice. See how easy? One approaches the candidate's picture and just punches in—not the nose, but the card.

A brain is a terrible thing to waste, if you have one. Now, we rally round the flack boys, we rally once again, shouting the battle cry of "free-dumb."

As in the great Civil War, when the nation was torn apart by war, we must have learned a lesson. "All for one and one for all." Let's have unity, and let us formulate a plan to unite the two parties into one, and call it the "Repo-Dems."

Forsooth, we must use the great Lincoln. Link-on—gosh, how clever.

My system will eliminate the silly running around the country kissing babies, or kissing women. Do so, but careful of the dentures.

Jaws, let's put out the lights and go to bed.

Are We Running Dry, or How Dry I Am

Water, water everywhere
And not a drop in my sink
If we don't soon get some
We will be off the brink

This is no laughing matter. By the gift of water we nourish and sustain all living things. We could experience a really catastrophic condition when all nations begin the great drought periods. Unless aroused citizens in this country and other countries wake up to this situation, we will be caught short.

The conflict between humanity's growing thirst and the projected supply of usable water could result in the most devastating natural disaster in recorded history.

Extra: The world's population of more than 5.9 billion will double in the next 50 to 90 years. The water supply is constant. Compounding these facts is the grim reality that water consumption is rising as fast as the world population is rising. You do not have to be an Einstein to understand that we are headed towards a calamity.

We question the fear of a water shortage, when we have an abundance of streams, lakes, rivers, and all sorts of water supplies. But with the tremendous population explosion, we require more water.

In California, Owens Lake was tapped to supply water to Los Angeles, and now only a dry lake bed remains.

What can you do to help? First, take the pledge: I will eliminate all the wasteful flushing of the toilet, which consumes five or more gallons daily. I will save this daily expression in a large bucket or jar, and then at the end of the day dispose of it by flushing it down the drain. You might place a sign on the bathroom which reads "We aim to please, hope your aim is good." Just calculate the number of gallons that you can save each year by this exercise.

With the elimination of jocularity, let's be serious, and remember that other countries are not that fortunate to have a large amount of water available as we have here in America.

Don't try this at home: When the astronauts are in their space station, they cannot carry enough water to last them for any real length of time, so their urine is recirculated and used again as drinking water. Ugh.

Ho-Hum. Don't be so smug. In the earth's plan, there will some day be a water shortage, unless mankind becomes kinder, and devises methods to eliminate this problem. While we here in America may not understand its importance, other countries like India and Pakistan might just go to war to keep the supply of water flowing over their borders.

Let's stop for a brief moment and ponder the amount of water we use, in lawn watering, air conditioning, bathing, and multiple other wasted amounts of drinking water. Just flushing the toilet might consumer about five gallons, which could be used for more useful purposes instead. For example, spray only one side of your body each time you shower. When your shower is complete and the water is collected in the bathtub, get a suction hose that will drain the water from the tub and collect it in a giant tub on the outside of the house for watering gardens. If you do that, ur-in.

Regarding my car, just before a rain I soap it up and then when it rains I have bright looking car. Swimming pools need quite an amount of water. Before the Great Depression, we collected rain water and used it to bathe, and the girls used this water to wash their hair, which made it exciting to run my fingers through their soft hair. Wow.

Horsie, keep your tail down. Many "tears" ago, when cars were not prevalent, there were a great number of horses, especially in New York, dispensing a Niagara-type inundation of watery displays, anytime and anywhere. So some genius, who made a scientific study called "urinology," used a mathematical quadrant to calculate the amount in gallons these horses exercised on their disposals each day. Believe me, this was a large amount of street smarts, while you waited for the completion of the endless spray. This could result in a "urin-nation."

An Electrifying Governor

Let's delve into the mysteries of governorship.

The general purpose of all government is "to establish justice, insure domestic tranquility, provide for the common defense, promote the general welfare, and secure the blessings of liberty."

During Christie Whitman's campaign for governor, I noticed the combatants were not conforming to "domestic tranquility" and were acting like a bunch of spoiled brats, vying for the governorship. Being an old "died-in-the-wool"—which has now turned to synthetics—I was of the opinion that all women's place was in the kitchen and home. Wow, a mistake in time saves nine.

This was the epitome of science, and also can be called "men-in-gitis," forsooth. Yes, I am a man, and still trying to prove it. Forget the ides of March, or the Alamo: just fear the selection of a president by a popular vote, for naught.

Each year, Sheriff Englehardt promotes a great picnic, which is held at one of the colleges. The troops gather for a good time, and the people have the opportunity to met new friends and just mingle.

Governor Whitman was invited to attend this annual picnic. And now we find her entering with all the excitement allotted to a queen. One of the first to meet her was my sister Mitzie. Good hand shakes, how are you, all the right modes. Number two was my brother Louis, a retired Baptist minister, who told the governor that he just arrived from Florida, just to see and shake hands as a form of welcome. The governor thanked him, with a whimsical smile, and continued on the path of friendliness. Now it was my turn. As she entered between a long and thick line of people, I shook hands with her and hoped for a firm rule in the state. A young lady behind me said that she was in a row that prevented her from shaking hands with the governor, so I immediately formed a great plan. I told her that if she would hold my hand, then I would shake hands with the governor and in that manner I would make her very happy. Little did I realize the emotional consequences this would create.

The hands were now in progress, but then it happened that there was an enormous electrical shock wave that reverberated through this connection. The audience stood in shock and silence, and after they gained some composure they raised their voices in a great uproar. The magic that had been created left the multitude in a happy frame of mind.

After Sheriff Englehardt recovered, the proud sheriff let "milady" through the nobles and the nobles with a "She made my day." The show did go on.

Dear Governor Whitman, please be careful whom you shake hands with.

Jewish Humor

The Prince of Laughter. First, let's call it "Jewish Wisdom." Let's face the facts, with all the suffering the Jews have experienced, suffering plagues and many adjustments, they came out on top. This is a tribute to their cherished sense of humor.

So it came to pass (who came to pass?) that papa was climbing the ladder of success, and decided to present his wife and daughter with a vacation gift. When they learned of this presentation, they were ecstatic. The vacation was completed and "all's well that ends well."

Mama always worried about papa, so now was the challenge to ensnare pop to go for his annual physical. He said no, she said yes, and finally he did go. (I can sympathize. It's like going for a haircut—oops, I'm due—in fact they never even gave me a lollipop.)

The curtain rises. I believe it was a staged act. Hold on, my fine feathered friend, this story is a lollapalooza. We are now at the doctor's office. Abe sits in silence, and views the various torture chamber implements that adorn the tables. Finally the nurse arrives, papers in hand, and announces that he is next. The execution continues. The doctor examines the nervous patient, who is led away gracefully. Not much flavor, just how now brown cow. Afterwards, he dons his clothes, adjusts his belt, and slowly saunters through the door to freedom.

Speaking of curtains, this past summer I saw a large truck pass with large letters that read "Let us do your drapes, otherwise it's curtains for you."

Abe arrives at home, where they give him a brave welcome. "So," his wife asks, "what did the doctor say?" Abe sits down with his head in his hands, as if the world is going to cave in. Mama again asks, "Why do you sit with the world's problems, tell me what he said."

Most reluctantly, he mentions that the received a thorough physical, but he became frightened when the doctor said that all is fine, but "I must tell you that you have a fluckey."

Boy, that did it, what shall we do? His wife tells him that she will get to the bottom of this problem. Sadie goes through the entire realm of friends who are well acquainted with medical problems, and also contacts the butcher, the baker, and the candlestick maker, but no one can explain what a "fluckey" is. As a last resort, she says, "Abie, go back to the doctor and let him explain what a 'fluckey' is and that will end it all."

So we are looking into the eyes of dedication, frustration, and finally medication. He goes back to the doctor very reluctantly. At the office of the doctor, he again observes the many tools of the doctor's trade, but just then the nurse calls him and he sees the doctor. The doctor takes one look at him and says that he looks like he was hit by a train. The doctor asks what could have happened since the last visit. Abe explains that he had a disease. "Who told you that terrible thing," the doctor asks.

"Why, you did," Abe replies. "You said that I had a "fluckey."

"Oh my gosh," the doctor said. "I told you that you 'got off lucky'!"

The Passaic Avenue Incident

Clifton, New Jersey. Time to trim the hedges. A brave soul, I gathered my equipment, which consisted of a mere hedge cutter, affixed the cord, and began fanning the cutter in a sweeping motion. For the time being, all went well, until oops! the cord got in the way of my swatches and pow! the cord was severed. Don't go away, because this cut line also activated a fuse to blow in the main fuse box, and who knows where it disconnected the current line. Behold.

Here on Passaic Avenue, near the cemetery, I live happily with my cocker spaniel, who acts a good friend as well as a fine watchdog, with only a few accidents along the way. All else is very quiet.

The front porch is encased in glass, which gives me a view of the New York skyline. What better place to enjoy my solitude than this place. Enough, onward with the story. Linger now.

Except for a few night calls by some birds and an occasional horn-blowing idiot, all seems peaceful. But I spoke too soon.

Around two in the morning, my faithful guard erupted into a fierce bark. This was accompanied by his continuous running from the rear inside door to the front porch. I slid out of bed and reached for my trusty revolver.

I entered the porch, only to note that a young lady was attempting to enter the porch. She was screaming and banging on the door and yelling for me to let her in. Remember, the fuse had cut the light off on the porch, so all I could see was her blurred figure. Being a good "crime watcher," I was reluctant to let her in.

The next best thing is to call 911, and in a flurry the police were there, coming up the steps. One officer, in a semi-shocked voice said, "By gosh, she is absolutely naked." Quickly he applied his coat to cover her figure, and as I bravely stepped out of my domain the officer called my attention to all her clothes that were strewn about on the lower landing of the steps.

She told the office in a quivering voice that she had met two men at one of the bars in Passaic (although any bar could be barbaric), and they were so nice, and when they offered to drive her home they passed many houses and since she did not acknowledge their good intentions, she was tossed out bodily after they disrobed her. All she wanted to do was to go home and rest. Her story was that they had a good time at the bar, and who would ever think that they were of that type, but it did not turn out that way. She cried bitterly and had learned her lesson and would tell her friends to be on the alert for these really nice fellows.

These true stories happen all across the country. There is rape, murder, kidnapping, and an assortment of foul plays. A lesson learned is a lesson earned. Take care.

Cow Dynamics

As kids, we sang this song:
> *Won't you wait*
> *By the old white gait*
> *Won't you wait*
> *Till the cows come home*
> *(1920)*

With the lowing of the cattle as they swish through the tall grass, but later on a sunny day, which enhances our story with bovine instinct, we present a tale of udder nonsense.

So it came to pass, on a knoll stood our friend good old Ferdinand the bull. He paused and surveyed the landscape. He slowly walked over to the edge and peered down at some lady cows. He had an urge to merge. Most bulls are bullish, and he was no exception. So let's look into the romance of the Bullgarian character.

The encyclopedia says that "the cow is more valuable to man than any other quadruped, with the exception of the horse."

Charles Dickens once wrote:

> *If civilized people were ever to lapse into the worship of animals, the cow would certainly be their goddess. What a blessing is the cow. She*

is the mother of beef, the source of butter, the original cause of cheese, to say nothing of shoe horns, hair combs, and upper leather. A gentle animal, ever yielding creature, who has no joy in her family affairs which she does not share with man. We rob her of her children, that we may rob her of her milk. We only care for her when the robbing my be perpetuated.

So here on the farm, the plot "Dickens." Again we saunter to the edge of the low bluff, so that Ferdinand can visually enhance his better pasture. The cows below were grazing peacefully and chewing not the rag but their cud. Back at the knoll, he peered down the slight incline and raised himself to his full height, pawed the ground, snorted a bit, and slowly descended. Then he increased his speed and was headed for the brown cow, which seemed to be the prettiest. Happy days are here again. Full speed ahead. Nothing can stop this roaring engine.

But his calculations went awry, because he did not notice the barbed wire fence between the cow and himself. Then in an instant he saw the fence. Holy Toledo! (Into the alley and over the fence, I got the pail, who's got ten cents?) Ferdinand did not entirely clear the entire fence, resulting in causing mayhem and losing his family jewels. He pulled up short, faced the brown cow, and exclaimed "How Now Brown Cow?"

Each climatic change deserves another. The family veterinarian performed what seemed impossible. He reconstructed the injured jewel, and the bull became bullish again.

In the future, Ferdinand was careful of all defences and lived a life of polygamy, bovinity personified.

A Marriage Expert-Tease

We can scrutinize that a young female child might observe that there is a pronounced difference between a male and the female counterpart. Come rain or shine, here begins the metamorphosis, as barefooted pregnant we could render a series of explanations, but we must forge ahead like the blacksmith, and above all we must guard against the present day slogan, Have more fun in bed.

Let's look at this miracle, childbirth. I was devastated when I learned that the stork was now obsolete. For shame. And now we have a complicated procedure of "push and pull" let alone the myriads of bottles and diapers and drug-related paraphernalia, which turns into the "witching hour." Then again, we are introduced to the elbow testing, up at night, shut 'em up, many trips to the doctor, formulas, baby kissing, and heaven knows what. I got you, babe.

Let's follow the little footsteps to, you guessed it, the closet. Here is the realm, the kingdom of the older sister. Our lover begins the transformation of knightly or naughty deeds. We can also call this the hatching egg. Also, evolution personified. Here lies an arduous rank and armor. Here is an example of a little one in the glorified position to indulge to its utmost the study of everlasting beauty.

First we will open the closet. Wow, what have we here. High heeled shoes, long drape-like gowns, look here, lots of belts, funny wigs, containers, jewels, other unmentionables. Okay, let's try a few things on. Boy, the kids next door would eat their hearts out if they saw me now. Now armed to the teeth, she sallies forth in all her glory (into the alley and over the fence, I got the pail, who's got ten cents). Let's continue. She saunters into the hallway and meets her dear wretched brother, who surveys the masquerade, lifts up his flailing arms, which denotes hopelessness for this clown, symbolic of a gruesome figure roaming the English flats, seeking the lost souls. Our lady executes a quick retreat, muttering that he is a knave, with ill-gotten gains. She is quite perturbed, and he is not worth the effort to become interested, for he is redundant and forever hold your peace. He is not one to appreciate the glamour she has concocted. By gone, ye sinner.

The curtain falls, and rises on the plot, and we meet the former child prodigy. Our little pimpernel has been transformed into a gracious lady. The finishing school has resulted in her every cherished moment, and she is now ready to reach her long sought endeavors.

We can predict that she will meet the massive surge of the animal called man. If she can keep her head, while others are losing theirs and blaming it on her, then she will not be called "header-hopper."

Schlumping around, these aimless men carouse around all avenues of indulgence, these men have incorporated the use of telescopic visions to enable them to cast furtive glances, or redress, undress, and render the victim into a hopeless state of clothes-lessness.

Santa Claws—Sci-Fi

A few years ago, I had the pleasure of talking to Santa. He is like a barometer in predicting the weather. He was accustomed to inclement weather. He was like the proverbial mailman whose slogan was, Neither heat nor sleet nor athletes feet nor gloom of night.

In our conversation, Santa was very upset because one of his reindeer was ill, and he would find it difficult to go on his yearly trip without a full complement of deer. I listened to the sad story, and I immediately went into action. I contacted a friend in Deer-born, Michigan, who listened to me with endeering interest. He said that he had a deer in mind that was very healthy and could do the job. He went on to say that this deer was sound of mind and body. This was a request of Santa's in any deer.

The deer finally arrived and Santa was quite pleased. What shall we name him? Well, I said with a sly smile, you have Dunder and Blitzen so why not name him "Computer"? Santa said, I don't mean to offend you, but is he docile? Quickly I answered, "No meg-oh-bites."

Santa loaded up the sleigh and hitched up the reindeer, but as he was ready to leave he noticed that the new deer was "computing." Just before leaving he noticed that his wife was very nervous. He put his arms around her and said, "Now Dot, remain calm. Dot, calm."

His impatient reindeer just awaited the word from Santa. Santa mounted the sleigh, put on his seatbelt, and yelled "Away!" Then whisking over land and sea, he was ready for the Christmas adventure. He made a wide turn, selected his first house, and activated his snow dispenser, which consisted of twin exhaust pipes located in the rear of the sleigh, and cleared the roof for a safe landing. He approached the chimney with his expander, and watched the chimney expand, good for a jolly fat fellow. He climbed down the chimney.

Santa carefully sets the gifts on the table. Unbeknownst to him, while he arranges the gifts a little boy loiters in the room's shadows. He has his camera and is going to register all Santa's activities. Lo and behold, the boy's mother enters the room. Santa immediately embraces her and kisses her, while the boy notes, "I saw Santa kissing Mommy." Quite a turn, eh? This will live on in the hearts of mankind.

After the ball is over, and all the presents are distributed, Santa arrives home and relaxes in his giant easy chair, and Dot supplies him with the nectar of the gods. Dot gives him a low-calorie martini. His jolly elves receive a vacation at Disney World.

There is a knock on the door. Santa receives a telegram, he is summoned to Washington. Reading on, he is told to report for a review of the "kissing mommy" scene. Can you imagine our Santa becoming involved in such a horrible episode? He wonders how anyone saw him in the kissing action.

He bids the gang goodbye, takes a plane, and arrives in Washington. He goes to the high court. The situation is complex and in turmoil.

The prosecutor has all the necessary evidence and tells the jury about the incident. But how could anyone blame Santa, for he has a record pure as the flying snow. He also is known to live a Claustered life.

The games begin. The prosecutor begins the evidence and tells the jury that at the first home Santa visited, and while arranging the presents, a figure lurking in the shadows was taking pictures. He detested Santa for not giving him gifts, for Santa knew that this kid was intolerable. The prosecutor now asked the boy, in his own words, to tell it like it was. What really transpired in your home that night or eve of Christmas ever?

He asks Santa, Did you kiss the defendant that night? Santa sys, No I did not. The boy stands up and yells, Liar, liar, liar. The boy produces the camera, and there he is, big as life, the perpetrator—Santa.

After some tea and crumpets, the jury returns to their seats. The judge now addresses the jury and asks, How sayeth thou?

The foreman stands amidst the shocked people and reads the jury's verdict. We the jury, being in good health and paying 20% to our credit card culprits, find the defendant . . .

My sister shook me and said, Wake up, Ed.

Tarzan's Adventure in the Pyramids

Edgar Rice Burroughs wrote the novel *Tarzan of the Apes* in 1915. As kids, we emulated Tarzan, swinging from branches and vines, under the supervision of our patents. We built tree houses and gave the famous Tarzan yell, although not with any great volume (it frightened the birds away). We also beat our chests, boys only (no social security).

Let's do a 'jungle peek," and envision the depth of the jungle, with its many cries, growls, yells, and jungle inhabitants. Ah, there is Tarzan now, swinging above us on high, one vine to another. We will endeavor to bring the untold, unwritten, and undulated story of his adventures in the pyramids with Edgar Rice Burroughs, who could burrow, and Tarzan, who could climb to great heights and had a keen sense of smell

Tarzan was really a swinger. There he goes, vining towards what he calls home. There is the tree house, he swings on the last tree and lands right on his front porch. Jane is waiting for him, with the usual unadulterated gin martini, two olives. He asks for another and another. "Hold it," says Jane, "what are you doing? Why so many drinks?" "Well, Jane," he says, "it's a jungle out there."

After telling Jane about his experiences, he must meet the chief of the local village and plan the future of the tribe. Tarzan bids Jane well being, and knows that while he is gone there will not be any monkeying around, but only ape protection.

So what type of secret mission has been entrusted to Edgar Rice Burroughs and Tarzan? The committee in charge of the pyramids realized that not all the treasure had been found, and they required someone to investigate the various crypts and reveal the operations of the many tunnels and passages, and the knowledge of its cantilevers. The committee was aware of the special talents of both theses men. Tarzan had a keen sense of smell and is a great climber, and Burroughs could burrow. What a team. There have been scientists, grave robbers, mummy takers, and the whole lot of sneak thieves, but still no one could break the code of the magnificent pyramids. Many stories told of some fatal events that have caused the deaths of a few who dared to exploit the tombs. Both men knew of these tales but were accustomed to unknown tragedies and could cope with any of them.

With all the digging and scientific research, the builders of the pyramids left no indication of any contrivances to determine its method of architecture. Again we seem to have two insignificant human beings like Tarzan and Burroughs who are now making an attempt to enter the unknown and undiscovered areas of the pyramids' enclosure. It was with a great effort on the part of Burroughs that they learned of a secret passage that was as yet not discovered. These ancient builders had great engineers, who have confused the great minds of today. Rumors have been concocted that some alien people from outer space visited our planet and devised these monuments. Since some of the men entering the pyramids were infected or died of mysterious causes, people assumed that there was a curse on all intruders.

They finally discovered a small entrance as indicated by Burroughs, who removed any obstacle that was in their approach to the hidden treasures. Some passages were small, others required climbing over, while they found the hidden levers that moved the great and heavy masonry. When they operated the levers the immense stone slab began to rotate, and exposed another great room. Some of these slabs of granite were designed to kill a person if any object was moved that would expose the hidden treasure room.

This was an arduous trip of crawling, shoving, and operating various levers to gain access to the throne of the king. On occasion, as the stone slab was turning inward, Tarzan detected a foul odor that was unfamiliar to jungle smells. This ageless tomb had its history and both men were about to find its mystery. (Slowly I turn. . . .)

Both men rejoiced to have been the first to discover this ancient treasure. Now was the time to

inform their peers of the spectacular success. However, great care must be taken to prevent any ambi-
tions characters from accessing the tomb (oh joy)

All the found treasures were removed safely
and undetected, by trusted members of the pyramids' constituents. Burroughs left the project and
headed home. Tartan lingered for a while to insure
that all was removed, and slipped out.

We now see Tarzan exit the pyramid and
climb up to its utmost peak, stand tall, raise his arms
up towards the sky, and in the fashion that only Tarzan can execute, in a roaring yell proclaim, "This entire project sphinx." Jungles away.

Wops Redundant

Immigrants, people coming from other countries to America, included many of our grandparents. For example, my parents came from Hungary in 1894, although not on the same ship.

Just the other evening, I saw an interesting account of the Immigration complex at Ellis Island. The process of immigration was to determine who would enter the United States, therefore they were questioned, examined, and also asked if any relatives could take them in and get them started, to make adjustments easier. There were strict check-ups as to any criminal records and diseases that could make them return to their native land. The immigrants who had no place to go were placed in hotels.

President Roosevelt said, "We all came from immigrants that were here to seek a better life for themselves and their families."

All immigrants who entered through Ellis Island were called "Wops." Few people knew the meaning of the word and suffered shame when they called the Italians "wops." The truth is that every person who entered the United States through Ellis Island was called a "wop," with meant "without official papers."

Transformations: Around the year 2000, the nationality of young people seemed to have blended them into what we call American Folks. When someone tells you that he is a true American, check his wampum belt and arrows, and no more bragging.

A Knight to Remember

This is the prelude to G minor.

This is the story of Clinton, the knight of the road. He must always remember to be prepared so that someday he will become king, when the king, his father, passes into the great beyond.

In a quiet glade on the edge of the kingdom, two knights square off for combat. One is defending the land of his forebears, the other the honor of his crest. The other warrior screams defiance and is assured in his right and divine providence.

Swords clash, armor rattles, the defender, Prince Clinton, scores a direct hit to the chest, and the other knight falls to his knees in defeat.

A romantic scene plucked out of the middle ages. The noble knaves cheer their master, who bows in great humility. The multitude, like our sports fans, become paralyzed with joy. There is dancing in the streets, the jugglers juggle, the singers sing, and the pickpockets are picking. More, the group is grouping. The king's subjects remember what the king said, which was, "We will not tolerate any leaks in this kingdom." Forsooth, the land is becoming eroded. So it came to pass.

It is now time to set aside the frivolity, and concentrate on the rigors of mortis. At any time, we can find Prince Clinton hard at work, tuning up his steed, sharpening his sword, and all the necessary gadgets that are now required by prince charming.

With the passage of time, the king becomes quite ill. The doctors believe that he has "skivers of the livers" (don't ask). In just a few years later the king becomes de-com-pooped. That is how the poem came to pass:

> *In days of old, when knights were bold*
> *and toilets not yet invented*
> *They left their loads upon the roads*
> *and walked away contented*

Prince Clinton worked all his kinks and ways, and thus was ready to gain the crown whenever the opportunity presented itself. He is now ready to fill his father's shoes (check for explosives) and work his way to being crowned. The new king is a very strong man, and has finally reached adultery, or, as the army put it, Section 8. In other words, he is not too well wrapped.

All subjects are overjoyed, has not our king slain the dragons and dragged them back to the castle? On his way back, he cell phones so that they should get ready for the hozen-feffer mit sour-kraut. Prelude to G minor. Our stalwart prince, well adorned, walks slowly toward the parapet, but his servants begin the role of the presentations of credit cards which are strewn in the path. It is his big day.

He now ascends to the parapet, ready with his prepared speech.

"I promise you, that someday you and I, will
take our love, together to some sky . . .

"Now hear this, we must remember the wise
sayings of my father, your king. Long live the king.
He said that regardless of what other kings prescribe
to their subjects, for example regardless of the politi-
cally correct campaign other kingdoms believe in, we
will not permit leaks in our courtyard, which creates
fissures in our walkways."

While Clinton speaks, a loud clamor rises, as
the knights and peasants enter the courtyard. The
question is, why was it possible for the prince to follow his father's domain without fanfare? The prince
reveals the secret of his successful venture. He said
that he spent one night at the Holiday Inn.

We wish our great king Godspeed. Let no
man admonish it, Les we forget, but not Ed.

Sports

In 1618, King James I declared that dancing, archery, and may games were lawful after divine services, but prohibited bear baiting, bull baiting, bowling, and interludes. In the state of savagery, man's life depended on his agility in running, jumping, climbing, and throwing of projectiles. The civilization of ancient Greece considered prowess in the arts of speed and endurance, and the entire population partook. In recent years, we have established a renewal of these sports, as well as the marathon races, which cover the distance of 26 miles and 385 yards.

The following pathological story is not for the faint of heart, nor for the godlike reverence placed upon a plain human who runs around the court or field.

So fasten your seatbelts, get your soda and Cracker Jacks and peanuts, but don't pay attention to the pretty girl sitting next to you, for I just saw her husband buying something to eat and he shall return. Instead, pay full attention to the game. Don't be distracted by earthly things. Baseball is a godly thing and should not be taken too lightly.

You miss catching the bag of peanuts, yet you bawl out the catcher for not drawing in the ball to create a strike.

The coach shoos the players out of the dugout—this was named after the groundhog that saw its shadow. After a few push-ups, the saints go marching in. Each player takes his place. Somewhere in the background, some fool yells, Kill the umpire. However, there is no cause for that, for they haven't started playing.

The batter now lined up gets in some foreplay. He grips two bats, swings them around, spits on the ground, adjusts his hamstrings, and faces the pitcher, but also keeps an eye on the catcher, who by this time is sending coded messages to the pitcher. The ball comes in neat passage over the plate, he slams the ball high into left field, runs to first, second, and finally stops at third after a grand slide. He quickly turns to view the multitude, to learn of their displeasure. They point at him and in unison yell in a voluminous thunder, Go home, go home, go home. Why should he go home, I ask you, when he wants to play baseball.

Silence prevails over the gentry (people of good birth or breeding). One of the outstanding players is brought forth to symbolize this player's good fortune, for he is being traded to another outstanding team. He is led to the home plate, encircled by the pitcher, the catcher, no, not the candlestick maker, but the coach, who proudly announces that he is now being led away to join forces with another team that may someday beat the daylights out of this "giveaway team." Yes, he will bollisk the pants offen them (baseball talk). The anointed player slowly leaves the sacrificial altar. With furtive glances he wipes the tears and wonders, Why me?

Breathes there a man with soul so dead, who never to himself has said, I'll watch the game until they pronounce me dead. How deceased.

I go back to Babe Ruth's time. I was born and bread, and liked it with butter and jelly. Let's formulate the area of baseball. Yes, a sport of kings. They watched the crystal ball while the good wife tended to her knitting. Even if she dropped a few. In most sports, we develop great bodies, and develop baseball "bat-ah-toe-ma." How veinacular.

All of today's sports are based on the Roman Coliseum concept. There mayhem took place, the gladiators pinned a victim down while the bloodthirsty Romans turned their thumbs up or down. We have a throwback of this in the finger concept. We call this a "fingered gesture" or onslaught. Don't be alarmed when you are presented with the finger. Just remember the doctor will navigate the rod wisely.

Retrogression. It is better to have lost a game than never to have played at all. Without the cheerleaders, there won't be any attire to admire. Into the valley of death rode the ten thousand.

Let's veer off to the right and consider the sports widows. A dauntless surge of pulchritude (beauty). The "messter" confronts the "boob tube" with sandwiches, beer, and an attitude that is not worth viewing. The sports widow has a boring day, and must be attentive to this blob of stick-to-it-ness? He is very aware that the players are not conforming to his plan of attack. He yells, screams, pounds on the table and sez, Dammit, give me another beer.

I visited my nephew during a well-heeled game on Sunday. He was about 18, and at this age you know it all. You also know that you will live for-ever. He watched the game very carefully, and began yelling that the player should not have left the base, only to be counted out. Well, this was my time to adjust the game. I gave the phone to him, and with a disturbed look he asked me who it was. I told him it was the manager of the game. He heard you yelling about this misguided player and called to let you sim-ply chastise him.

A lesson was not learned, for this prevails throughout the land. In basketball, now we have a "dunk" play where the player jumps up to at the basket, hangs in there for a moment, and dunks the ball into the basket. Well, my dear forlorn basketeers who have no more pride left, I do tell you that when we played some time around 1930 if we hung on to the basket, we would have really become a "basket case." Allegro.

To alleviate tension, I asked a friend of mine if he knew the two girls, Lucy and Carrie. Well, he asked, Lucy and Carrie who? So it came to pass that I mentioned that the were Lucy Bowels and Carry Paper. Laugh and the world laughs with you, cry and you cry alone.

Baseball, The Good Old Days

How well I remember the good old days. We admired all the baseball players, and some were more like heroes. At the time I was just 12, I also remember that when we bought a pair of shoes we received a baseball bat or glove.

Babe Ruth and the Yankees recall the days when there were no TVs and not many planes. At that time, when a plane went overhead all the kids ran out into the street and yelled, "Air-o-plane, air-o-plane." Those were the days, when there were no men on the moon and the only major sport was baseball.

When I was still a young man, a very good friend of mine, Walter Stikeman, was a close friend of Babe Ruth's. The Babe autographed a baseball for Walter's young son. It was just a few years later that the boy died. Stikeman offered the ball to me. However, I suggested he give the ball to his grandchildren. There for the grace of the game go I.

As an article in the newspaper pointed out, old fashioned sports and a slower way of life produced inventions that were adopted to civilian use and changed the way we live and amuse ourselves. Is our way better than the ways in past times, when New Jersey's Silk Socks or other semi-pro clubs played ball on a Sunday afternoon? Is ours a better way than a trip up the Hudson, or down the bay on a steam boat, or a trolley to Coney Island or Rockaway? Is a ride to the seaside in a sedan a better way to woo a maid than a cruise by boat past Westside park on the Passaic River? A buggy ride at twilight was infinitely better than motoring. One could wrap the reins around the dashboard and tend to more important things than directing the horse, who already knew the way home. He also had eyes to keep him out of trouble.

Is today a better way than in 1923, when the Hudson Trolley whisked a couple from Paterson to the Palisades in 25 minutes? The fact is that ten minutes by street car from the other side of Passaic could mean thrills at Fairyland Park. Carodos supermarket stands where the carousel, the whip, and the grotto of fun at Fairyland once stood. Do we really have things that good these days?

Golf

Good golf. Anticipation, preparation, and dedication. Fore: the malady of sports. Ready the iron, tote that pail, and hit the trail. Boy, what fun. Like the ladies of the lake, great attire, short shorts, high cuts, low cuts, no cuts. The caddies caddy, the golfers golfer, and now keep an eye on the ball. Quite spirited, eh what?

The golfer places the ball on the tee, but not the balls cup. The ball sits on the tee and muses, Wow, here I am on a tee, like some pedestal. Like a king. He looks up at the sun and takes in all the glorious delights of the day. What did I do to deserve this? Is it platitude or latitude? Above his head, there appears a shadow as he sits on his throne, which he does not realize is the golfer, getting ready to commit "harris-carious."

Ah-ha, it is a practice shot, which parts my hair. I became very concerned, the next one is the real one.

Wham, bam, thank you m'am. This sends me out in space, and I must do something. Ah, now I come to a screeching halt. Am I safe? Hell, no. A menacing hand reaches in and drags me out. No screaming will aid me. Now what? Well, I see. It's tee time again.

Another direct hit. Again I am numb with fear. There is no escaping from this swift injustice. Here I go, down the beautiful lawn, and heading straight for the pond. The water engulfs, it seems that it is time for recycling.

An alien appears. Like the axe file on the cutting edge, Tee-a-dor Golf, a brother of the hapless golf ball, who has experienced the trial by fire. Remember, he was slammed with force into the pond, but we are not aware of his plight. Tee-a-dor Golf felt that he must retaliate for the good of the golf world. He is an alien, and at will he cannot be seen. Trial and terror. Myron Holman, the ardent golfer with his father Holman, Sr., places the golf ball on the tee. (Shhhhh. He does not know that he has become the victim of perilous "golf-finnions," forsooth.) Junior steps up to the plate, swings the club precariously, and after a few strokes slams the ball thither and yon. Tee is ready for the flight. Don't consider this preposterous. Like the pyramids, the mystery of its origin and structure may never be known. Now, don't turn up your nose, because you are now part of this charade.

Tee laughs all the way to the hole. Please stand by for the latest feature.

"Alpha and omega." Tee, now with a sneer on his rubberized features, will now demonstrate his prowess. Clouds form, a hush falls over the golf course, flashes of lightning, a few strikes, over the manicured lawn. A golfer yells "Fore," fore this he will suffer. Junie, don't leave me now.

The beautiful lawn now turns brown and lifeless, an errant ball strikes a player, all golf balls decompose, the sand traps turn into a quagmire. The water trap dries up. Golf carts explode and Tee, with his rubberband arms folded, laughs like Boris the Car-loss. President Roosevelt sends a telegram which reads "This is a day of infamy."

I flash out my cell phone, and contact Myron. He tells me to come over because Paul Harvey wants us all to see the amazing find he discovered. Naturally, this was just "after the ball was over."

We later hear his exciting radio comments, as he relates stories of unusual events. Well, now he explains the golf course scene, where a player hit the ball into one of the holes, reached down to retrieve a few balls, more balls, more balls, there seemed to be no end to this phenomenal event. To his dismay, this seemed endless. He became alarmed and notified the office. The application of the backhoe discovered hundreds of golf balls. It was assumed that at first there was a small hole that eventually grew larger. As Paul Harvey would say, "Now the story can be told."

This is a true story, which occurred in October 1998.

Tee-a-dor exclaimed victory. Tee-a-dor, in all his glory, found his brother who was still alive. He had a "bounce-back" composition. They had a ball watching the confused golfers run astray. Naturally, they created the hole where all the balls gathered to attend a great meeting.

The writer muses, All is not lost for the golfer is our greatest anticipater for the "hole in one." Swing in there, while we peasants run around dodging cars, the golfer views the majestic greens, sunshine, and a "godly spirit." Amen. Many of our greatest minds gather for business adventures, and we have business and pleasure combined.

As the priest in M*A*S*H would say jocularly, 'tis a "hole new story." So Myron Sr. and Jr., I bid thee godspeed, stay out of the sun, keep the lightning rod rigid, stay clear of trees in the storm, wear proper shoes, throw the umbrella away, and listen to me. If at first you don't succeed, try chewing it.

The Other Sports

Tennis

Tennis, Anyone? Ah, 'tis a beautiful day. Prepare the great weaving match. No short comings, each will look their best. The players size each other up to determine her attire, any bumps, or short shorts? Tight fits? Hey, that's my line. The girls present a picture with their attire, and create a gate which does not present a defense.

The players, especially the girls, now become nervous. So I say, Dot calm. OK netter, they face each other, shake hands, and serve.

It is rumored that some of the greatest courtships have been conceived on the net.

This only boils down to the fact that the game is not only a racket, but also has some strings attached.

> _Little players on the net_
> _You be sure I'll place a bet_
> _I know I'll win just by nerve_
> _And if I do, it's time to serve._

Cricket

Don't confuse this game with our own Jiminy Cricket. The British national game Cricket goes back as far as 1685.

Two teams of eleven players meet on level turf with two "wickets" twenty-two yards apart. A wicket consists of three twenty-inch-high stumps with two pieces of wood (bails) across the top. The stumps are close together enough so that a ball cannot pass between them.

The cricket bat is thirty inches long, with a twenty inch blade above a ten inch handle about the thickness of a baseball bat. The cricket ball is hard leather.

An umpire stands near each wicket, but only gives a decision when appealed to by a team. The team that takes the bat posts one batsman at each wicket.

The bowler bowls the ball against the wicket opposite him, which the batsman defends by stopping the ball with his bat or sending it to another part of the field. The other players are deployed around the playing field, and must catch or stop the ball with bare hands.

After sending the ball onto the field, the batsman runs to the opposite wicket and changes places with the other batsman. He scores a run by reaching the wicket before the ball is returned. It the opposing team gets the ball and knocks down the bails of the wicket before he gets there, the batsman is out

After six balls have been bowled to one end, the umpire calls "over" and another bowler bowls toward the opposite wicket.

Cricket is a game of "fair play," and no actions that would embarrass a player or hamper his ability to play well are tolerated. There have been calls to "spice up" the game in order to quicken the pace and add spectator interest, but players say that just "wouldn't be cricket."

The Wanderers cricket team, of the New York Metropolitan Cricket Association, plays on weekends in a park in Paterson, N.J. The West Indian immigrants who make up the team come from as far away as Brooklyn to join in the weekend matches.

A cricket in time save nine.

Football

While we all played the game, not all of us know the history of football, or should we say American Rugby. That name sounds strange, but it's probably what we should call this English game that the colonists brought to America. (To the rest of the world, "football" means soccer.)

Football, in one form or another, was played by the Greeks, the Romans, the Indians of North America, and Aboriginal people of many Pacific Islands. But the game got rules in the 1800s, and eventually became two different sports: rugby, which permits running with the ball, and soccer, which doesn't.

Early Virginia colonists brought the English game to America, and by the mid-1800s several colleges had begun to play. But games at Amherst, Brown, Harvard, Trinity, and Yale became so rough that the colleges prohibited the new sport. Princeton adopted the more refined English Association code, and the first intercollegiate game took place in 1860, between Princeton and Rutgers. Meanwhile, Harvard revived the sport using rugby-style rules and refused to play soccer-style. In 1875 a compromise was reached, and Harvard played Yale under rules that allowed running with the ball and hitting the ball with the hand. By the next year, all the colleges had agreed to play football under the original rugby rules.

Football is now the most popular sport in the United States, with more than 40 million people attending games and many millions more watching the games on television.

Soccer

Soccer may be the most popular sport on Earth. The official name of the game is "Association Football," after the London Football Association, which set down the first uniform rules in 1863. The slang name soccer came from the "soc" in association plus the popular British slang suffix "er" (rugby is often called "rugger").

Basketball

Basketball begin in 1891, when James Naismith of the Young Man's Christian Association placed an ordinary peach basket high up on a balcony railing in order to give athletes a relief from indoor calisthenics during the winter.

Today, basketball is played in more than one hundred and thirty countries.

We must salute this man for the wonderful game he invented, but we must pause and consider what he would have said if he saw these characters hang on the baskets. In the old days, if we had hung on the baskets as they do today, we would have become a "basket case."

The Midas Touch

I was propelled into writing this chapter by none other than my editor, Laura McCarthy of Silk Purse Editorial Services, who dared tackle my "mess-u-script." She said the stories of my family were great and she wished she had more of the same. Presto Digitalis.

This story involves Myron Holman and me, at the United States Signal Corps in Camp Crowder, Missouri.

I, Edward Kurtz, of normal health, was in charge of a barracks with about forty men. This one day, at the mess hall, I saw Myron at the table. He was a recruit in basic training. We immediately became friends.

"Hey, kid," I said, "let's go to the movies," which were in camp. Some time later, I asked him to go out of town so that he could meet some of my friends in towns nearby. We attended some of the local church affairs, where I lectured about the great need for Scouting, and how it would help young men to adjust to daily problems as well as to learn confidence.

I taught a class of slow speed code at five words a minute. Next they sent me to a high speed code class of 25 words a minute. Guess who was the instructor. Yes, Myron Holman.

My sister Libby decided to visit me on the post. Naturally, she met the good-looking Myron, and thus began my prediction of a fierce adventure. She met Mr. Larsen, the movie owner, and various others, which gave her and Myron an attitude to become fast friends. Time motivates. They finally decided to get married. Our dear friend Mr. Larsen decided to give them a wedding present and supplied the wedding feast as well as other monetary inclusions.

First let's talk about the "Midas Touch." A common figure of speech, I remember the story which was presented to the class. They said it was associated with the story of the mythical king. When a person is successful in whatever he undertakes, we say that he has the "Midas Touch."

Midas Touch--Myron Touch

Myron stayed on to teach code for about a year while I was assigned to a company of specialists that was shipped to England. Finally, he was flown to Germany and we kept in touch.

The war over, Myron, my sister, and Myron, Jr. (no middle name) moved into our house. At the time I worked at the Forstmann Woolen Company, and I obtained a job for Myron. Myron, Jr., was about seven and was loved by my sister Mitzie. In fact, they had their own "laughing place" in the hall stairway. They would sit there and scream with laughter. (Mitzie and I still use the same place.)

When the Forstmann mills closed, leaving thousands without jobs, Myron applied to the Shotmeyer Gasoline Co., while I sent my resumes to about fifteen plants. No luck—they said I was great in textile but not qualified in their companies' products. Next move, I went into the house painting business.

But the Myron Touch rides again. Year after year, Myron was promoted at Shotmeyer from common clerk to his current position as President. You say, what background did he require for this magnificent position? Reminds me of story about the meeting the president of a company had with the staff where he presented a young man who was then a plain worker. He told them that the young man had risen from the ranks, as foreman, supervisor, manager and now vice president. The young man bowed his head and said, "Thanks, Dad."

Let's muse. Shotmeyer came from Holland with a new pair of wooden shoes, and also worked his way up to being owner of the gas company. He did not like the "fancy pants lawyers" or businessmen around him, so that Myron fitted in the right position, a country boy who lived on a farm and worked in a lumber yard.

Midas Touch? You bet.

Paul

Esma is the loving and lovely wife of Paul Kurtz, son of the author. This chapter is especially written for the lonely girls and women in this great nation. Books are written that try to provide love and happiness. Don't waste your time. Just follow the escapades of one happy wife, who slowly nods her head in agreement.

Paul built a train that he can ride on. This required several years to complete. It is motivated by coal and steam. Paul belongs to a club that has created a large area of land which has tracks, rising bridges and gates, just a fun place. When the crowd has gathered, women and children, plenty of food, soda and beer, cake and cookies, Paul turns to Ezzie and asks, "Isn't this fun?" She nods her head in agreement.

Ladies, stand by your man if you can.

Next adventure. Paul has a thirty-foot Morgan sailboat, equipped with an inboard motor, which is great for windless days. Now, Paul and Ezzie drag all the necessary equipment to the wharf. The boat club he belongs to affords a pilot boat to take them to their boat. On one of these exciting trips, Ezzie almost fell overboard while hauling up the spinnaker (a large rounded sail set on a long light pole). Later, the boat suddenly swerved around and swept our heroine Ezzie overboard. Paul immediately turned the boat around and saved our little one, his wife. The day's ordeal over, they went back to the wharf and dragged their luggage back to the car. Paul embraced Ezzie and said, "Boy, we really had fun." She nodded her head. At first I thought it was the flies that did it, but then I realized she was trying to agree.

Paul also works on antique cars. What do you do when you have antique cars? Don't ask. We go to antique car shows. Paul works on these cars until they are ready to win ribbons or plaques. There are many of these car shows, and in fact Paul has many of these ribbons and plaques to store, for future memories. Walk slowly and carry a big stick. Ready for the car "shoe"—where is Ezzie? Come out, wherever you are. Sheepishly she enters the ring, ready to take on the great show. Off to the wizard of "ooze." And another award. Did I see a cynical smile? You be the judge.

Now, girls, you can see how marriage can make you happy. Just tag along, stand by your man, and the days of happiness are about due.

Mitzie

My sister Mitzie--Mathilda Kurtz Derringer—
got me my job at Forstmann Woolen Company,
where she worked as a supervisor.

In the past, Mitzie wrote a play for the
church, translated Hungarian to English, and sang in
the choir and at weddings. She studied voice, and
each Sunday I would take her into New York to sing
Hungarian songs on radio station WWRL.

Now at 93, she cooks, washes and irons
clothes, goes shopping, handles all the money, and
has some mean telephone conversations. She plans
her meals a month in advance. Mitzie recalls that she
never required any pills or had any medical problems. The doctor said he didn't know her secret, but
she should continue doing whatever she is doing.
She has had two eye implants, which I don't like because now see sees more of the things I should not
do.

You will recall that there were seven of us in
our family. Of the five kids, only my sister Mitzie
and I are left, she at 93 and little ol' me at 87.

Some people ask me if it's in my genes. I tell
them that I don't wear them.

Well, then, what is the secret of my longevity?
Listen up—if you don't laugh at my jokes there

won't be any longevity.

I trust that you have enjoyed the "Good Old Days." God bless.

Printed in the United States
23190LVS00001B/122